Zondervan Illustrated Bible Backgrounds Commentary

# Mark

## David E. Garland

### Clinton E. Arnold *general editor*

ZONDERVAN®

## About the Authors

General Editor:

*Clinton E. Arnold* (Ph.D., University of Aberdeen), professor and chairman, department of New Testament, Talbot School of Theology, Biola University, Los Angeles, California

Gospel of Mark:

*David E. Garland* (Ph.D., Southern Baptist Theological Seminary), associate dean for academic affairs and professor of Christian Scriptures, George W. Truett Theological Seminary, Baylor University, Waco, Texas

ZONDERVAN

*Mark*
Copyright © 2002 by David E. Garland

Requests for information should be addressed to:
Zondervan, 3900 *Sparks Dr. SE, Grand Rapids, Michigan 49546*

This edition: ISBN  978-0-310-52291-1

The Library of Congress cataloged the original edition as follows:

Zondervan illustrated Bible backgrounds commentary / Clinton E. Arnold, general editor.
        p.   cm.
    Includes bibliographical references.
    ISBN 13  978-0-310-27830-6
    1. Bible. N.T.—Commentaries.  I. Arnold, Clinton E.
BS2341.52.Z66 2001
225.7—dc21                                                              2001046801

*Interior design: Sherri L. Hoffman*

*Printed in the United States of America*

| | |
|---|---|
| SBLMS | Society of Biblical Literature Monograph Series |
| *SBLSP* | *Society of Biblical Literature Seminar Papers* |
| SBS | Stuttgarter Bibelstudien |
| SBT | Studies in Biblical Theology |
| *SCJ* | *Stone-Campbell Journal* |
| *Scr* | *Scripture* |
| *SE* | *Studia Evangelica* |
| *SEG* | *Supplementum epigraphicum graecum* |
| SJLA | Studies in Judaism in Late Antiquity |
| *SJT* | *Scottish Journal of Theology* |
| SNTSMS | Society for New Testament Studies Monograph Series |
| SSC | Social Science Commentary |
| SSCSSG | Social-Science Commentary on the Synoptic Gospels |
| Str-B | Strack, H. L., and P. Billerbeck. *Kommentar zum Neuen Testament aus Talmud und Midrasch* |
| TC | Thornapple Commentaries |
| *TDNT* | *Theological Dictionary of the New Testament* |
| *TDOT* | *Theological Dictionary of the Old Testament* |
| *TLNT* | *Theological Lexicon of the New Testament* |
| *TLZ* | *Theologische Literaturzeitung* |
| TNTC | Tyndale New Testament Commentary |
| *TrinJ* | *Trinity Journal* |
| *TS* | *Theological Studies* |
| TSAJ | Texte und Studien zum antiken Judentum |
| *TWNT* | *Theologische Wörterbuch zum Neuen Testament* |
| *TynBul* | *Tyndale Bulletin* |
| WBC | Word Biblical Commentary Waco: Word, 1982 |
| WMANT | Wissenschaftliche Monographien zum Alten und Neuen Testament |
| WUNT | Wissenschaftliche Untersuchungen zum Neuen Testament |
| YJS | Yale Judaica Series |
| *ZNW* | *Zeitschrift fur die neutestamentliche Wissenschaft und die Junde der alteren Kirche* |
| *ZPE* | *Zeischrift der Papyrolgie und Epigraphkik* |
| *ZPEB* | *Zondervan Pictorial Encyclopedia of the Bible* |

## 5. General Abbreviations

| | |
|---|---|
| ad. loc. | in the place cited |
| b. | born |
| c., ca. | circa |
| cf. | compare |
| d. | died |
| ed(s). | editors(s), edited by |
| e.g. | for example |
| ET | English translation |
| frg. | fragment |
| i.e. | that is |
| ibid. | in the same place |
| idem | the same (author) |
| lit. | literally |
| l(l) | line(s) |
| MSS | manuscripts |
| n.d. | no date |
| NS | New Series |
| par. | parallel |
| passim | here and there |
| repr. | reprint |
| ser. | series |
| s.v. | *sub verbo*, under the word |
| trans. | translator, translated by; transitive |

| | | | |
|---|---|---|---|
| HJP | History of the Jewish People in the Age of Jesus Christ, by E. Schürer | NCBC | New Century Bible Commentary Eerdmans |
| HTR | Harvard Theological Review | NEAE | New Encyclopedia of Archaeological Excavations in the Holy Land |
| HTS | Harvard Theological Studies | | |
| HUCA | Hebrew Union College Annual | | |
| IBD | Illustrated Bible Dictionary | NEASB | Near East Archaeological Society Bulletin |
| IBS | Irish Biblical Studies | | |
| ICC | International Critical Commentary | New Docs | New Documents Illustrating Early Christianity |
| IDB | The Interpreter's Dictionary of the Bible | NIBC | New International Biblical Commentary |
| IEJ | Israel Exploration Journal | NICNT | New International Commentary on the New Testament |
| IG | Inscriptiones graecae | | |
| IGRR | Inscriptiones graecae ad res romanas pertinentes | NIDNTT | New International Dictionary of New Testament Theology |
| ILS | Inscriptiones Latinae Selectae | NIGTC | New International Greek Testament Commentary |
| Imm | Immanuel | | |
| ISBE | International Standard Bible Encyclopedia | NIVAC | NIV Application Commentary |
| | | NorTT | Norsk Teologisk Tidsskrift |
| Int | Interpretation | NoT | Notes on Translation |
| IvE | Inschriften von Ephesos | NovT | Novum Testamentum |
| IVPNTC | InterVarsity Press New Testament Commentary | NovTSup | Novum Testamentum Supplements |
| JAC | Jahrbuch fur Antike und Christentum | NTAbh | Neutestamentliche Abhandlungen |
| JBL | Journal of Biblical Literature | NTS | New Testament Studies |
| JETS | Journal of the Evangelical Theological Society | NTT | New Testament Theology |
| | | NTTS | New Testament Tools and Studies |
| JHS | Journal of Hellenic Studies | | |
| JJS | Journal of Jewish Studies | OAG | Oxford Archaeological Guides |
| JOAIW | Jahreshefte des Osterreeichischen Archaologischen Instites in Wien | OCCC | Oxford Companion to Classical Civilization |
| JSJ | Journal for the Study of Judaism in the Persian, Hellenistic, and Roman Periods | OCD | Oxford Classical Dictionary |
| | | ODCC | The Oxford Dictionary of the Christian Church |
| JRS | Journal of Roman Studies | OGIS | Orientis graeci inscriptiones selectae |
| JSNT | Journal for the Study of the New Testament | OHCW | The Oxford History of the Classical World |
| JSNTSup | Journal for the Study of the New Testament: Supplement Series | OHRW | Oxford History of the Roman World |
| | | OTP | Old Testament Pseudepigrapha, ed. by J. H. Charlesworth |
| JSOT | Journal for the Study of the Old Testament | | |
| JSOTSup | Journal for the Study of the Old Testament: Supplement Series | PEQ | Palestine Exploration Quarterly |
| | | PG | Patrologia graeca |
| JTS | Journal of Theological Studies | PGM | Papyri graecae magicae: Die griechischen Zauberpapyri |
| KTR | Kings Theological Review | | |
| LCL | Loeb Classical Library | PL | Patrologia latina |
| LEC | Library of Early Christianity | PNTC | Pelican New Testament Commentaries |
| LSJ | Liddell, H. G., R. Scott, H. S. Jones. A Greek-English Lexicon | Rb | Revista biblica |
| MM | Moulton, J. H., and G. Milligan. The Vocabulary of the Greek Testament | RB | Revue biblique |
| | | RivB | Rivista biblica italiana |
| | | RTR | Reformed Theological Review |
| MNTC | Moffatt New Testament Commentary | SB | Sources bibliques |
| | | SBL | Society of Biblical Literature |
| NBD | New Bible Dictionary | SBLDS | Society of Biblical Literature Dissertation Series |
| NC | Narrative Commentaries | | |

# CONTENTS

# INTRODUCTION

All readers of the Bible have a tendency to view what it says through their own culture and life circumstances. This can happen almost subconsiously as we read the pages of the text.

When most people in the church read about the thief on the cross, for instance, they immediately think of a burglar that held up a store or broke into a home. They may be rather shocked to find out that the guy was actually a Jewish revolutionary figure who was part of a growing movement in Palestine eager to throw off Roman rule.

It also comes as something of a surprise to contemporary Christians that "cursing" in the New Testament era had little or nothing to do with cussing somebody out. It had far more to do with the invocation of spirits to cause someone harm.

No doubt there is a need in the church for learning more about the world of the New Testament to avoid erroneous interpretations of the text of Scripture. But relevant historical and cultural insights also provide an added dimension of perspective to the words of the Bible. This kind of information often functions in the same way as watching a movie in color rather than in black and white. Finding out, for instance, how Paul compared Christ's victory on the cross to a joyous celebration parade in honor of a Roman general after winning an extraordinary battle brings does indeed magnify the profundity and implications of Jesus' work on the cross. Discovering that the factions at Corinth ("I follow Paul . . . I follow Apollos . . .") had plenty of precedent in the local cults ("I follow Aphrodite; I follow Apollo . . .") helps us understand the "why" of a particular problem. Learning about the water supply from the springs of Hierapolis that flowed into Laodicea as "lukewarm" water enables us to appreciate the relevance of the metaphor Jesus used when he addressed the spiritual laxity of this church.

My sense is that most Christians are eager to learn more about the real life setting of the New Testament. In the preaching and teaching of the Bible in the church, congregants are always grateful when they learn something of the background and historical context of the text. It not only helps them understand the text more accurately, but often enables them to identify with the people and circumstances of the Bible. I have been asked on countless occasions by Christians, "Where can I get access to good historical background information about this passage?" Earnest Christians are hungry for information that makes their Bibles come alive.

The stimulus for this commentary came from the church and the aim is to serve the church. The contributors to this series have sought to provide illuminating and interesting historical/cultural background information. The intent was to draw upon relevant papyri, inscriptions, archaeological discoveries, and the numerous studies of Judaism, Roman culture, Hellenism, and other features of the world of the New Testament and to make the results accessible to people in the church. We recognize that some readers of the commentary will want to go further, and so the sources of the information have been carefully documented in endnotes.

The written information has been supplemented with hundreds of photographs, maps, charts, artwork, and other graphics that help the reader better understand the world of the New Testament. Each of the writers was given an opportunity to dream up a "wish list" of illustrations that he thought would help to illustrate the passages in the New Testament book for which he was writing commentary. Although we were not able to obtain everything they were looking for, we came close.

The team of commentators are writing for the benefit of the broad array of Christians who simply want to better understand their Bibles from the vantage point of the historical context. This is an installment in a new genre of "Bible background" commentaries that was kicked off by Craig Keener's fine volume. Consequently, this is not an "exegetical" commentary that provides linguistic insight and background into Greek constructions and verb tenses. Neither is this work an "expository" commentary that provides a verse-by-verse exposition of the text; for in-depth philo-logical or theological insight, readers will need to have other more specialized or comprehensive commentaries available. Nor is this an "historical-critical" commentary, although the contributors are all scholars and have already made substantial academic contributions on the New Testament books they are writing on for this set. The team intentionally does not engage all of the issues that are discussed in the scholarly guild.

Rather, our goal is to offer a reading and interpretation of the text informed by what we regard as the most relevant historical information. For many in the church, this commentary will serve as an important entry point into the interpretation and appreciation of the text. For other more serious students of the Word, these volumes will provide an important supplement to many of the fine exegetical, expository, and critical available.

The contributors represent a group of scholars who embrace the Bible as the Word of God and believe that the message of its pages has life-changing relevance for faith and practice today. Accordingly, we offer "Reflections" on the relevance of the Scripture to life for every chapter of the New Testament.

I pray that this commentary brings you both delight and insight in digging deeper into the Word of God.

*Clinton E. Arnold*
*General Editor*

# LIST OF SIDEBARS

## Mark

# LIST OF CHARTS

# ABBREVIATIONS

## 1. Books of the Bible and Apocrypha

| | |
|---|---|
| 1 Chron. | 1 Chronicles |
| 2 Chron. | 2 Chronicles |
| 1 Cor. | 1 Corinthians |
| 2 Cor. | 2 Corinthians |
| 1 Esd. | 1 Esdras |
| 2 Esd. | 2 Esdras |
| 1 John | 1 John |
| 2 John | 2 John |
| 3 John | 3 John |
| 1 Kings | 1 Kings |
| 2 Kings | 2 Kings |
| 1 Macc. | 1 Maccabees |
| 2 Macc. | 2 Maccabees |
| 1 Peter | 1 Peter |
| 2 Peter | 2 Peter |
| 1 Sam. | 1 Samuel |
| 2 Sam. | 2 Samuel |
| 1 Thess. | 1 Thessalonians |
| 2 Thess. | 2 Thessalonians |
| 1 Tim. | 1 Timothy |
| 2 Tim. | 2 Timothy |
| Acts | Acts |
| Amos | Amos |
| Bar. | Baruch |
| Bel | Bel and the Dragon |
| Col. | Colossians |
| Dan. | Daniel |
| Deut. | Deuteronomy |
| Eccl. | Ecclesiastes |
| Ep. Jer. | Epistle of Jeremiah |
| Eph. | Ephesians |
| Est. | Esther |
| Ezek. | Ezekiel |
| Ex. | Exodus |
| Ezra | Ezra |
| Gal. | Galatians |
| Gen. | Genesis |
| Hab. | Habakkuk |
| Hag. | Haggai |
| Heb. | Hebrews |
| Hos. | Hosea |
| Isa. | Isaiah |
| James | James |
| Jer. | Jeremiah |
| Job | Job |
| Joel | Joel |
| John | John |
| Jonah | Jonah |

| | |
|---|---|
| Josh. | Joshua |
| Jude | Jude |
| Judg. | Judges |
| Judith | Judith |
| Lam. | Lamentations |
| Lev. | Leviticus |
| Luke | Luke |
| Mal. | Malachi |
| Mark | Mark |
| Matt. | Matthew |
| Mic. | Micah |
| Nah. | Nahum |
| Neh. | Nehemiah |
| Num. | Numbers |
| Obad. | Obadiah |
| Phil. | Philippians |
| Philem. | Philemon |
| Pr. Man. | Prayer of Manassah |
| Prov. | Proverbs |
| Ps. | Psalm |
| Rest. of Est. | The Rest of Esther |
| Rev. | Revelation |
| Rom. | Romans |
| Ruth | Ruth |
| S. of III Ch. | The Song of the Three Holy Children |
| Sir. | Sirach/Ecclesiasticus |
| Song | Song of Songs |
| Sus. | Susanna |
| Titus | Titus |
| Tobit | Tobit |
| Wisd. Sol. | The Wisdom of Solomon |
| Zech. | Zechariah |
| Zeph. | Zephaniah |

## 2. Old and New Testament Pseudepigrapha and Rabbinic Literature

Individual tractates of rabbinic literature follow the abbreviations of the *SBL Handbook of Style*, pp. 79–80. Qumran documents follow standard Dead Sea Scroll conventions.

| | |
|---|---|
| *2 Bar.* | *2 Baruch* |
| *3 Bar.* | *3 Baruch* |
| *4 Bar.* | *4 Baruch* |
| *1 En.* | *1 Enoch* |
| *2 En.* | *2 Enoch* |
| *3 En.* | *3 Enoch* |
| *4 Ezra* | *4 Ezra* |

# INDEX OF PHOTOS AND MAPS

| | |
|---|---|
| 3 Macc. | 3 Maccabees |
| 4 Macc. | 4 Maccabees |
| 5 Macc. | 5 Maccabees |
| Acts Phil. | Acts of Philip |
| Acts Pet. | Acts of Peter and the 12 Apostles |
| Apoc. Elijah | Apocalypse of Elijah |
| As. Mos. | Assumption of Moses |
| b. | Babylonian Talmud (+ tractate) |
| Gos. Thom. | Gospel of Thomas |
| Jos. Asen. | Joseph and Aseneth |
| Jub. | Jubilees |
| Let. Aris. | Letter of Aristeas |
| m. | Mishnah (+ tractate) |
| Mek. | Mekilta |
| Midr. | Midrash I (+ biblical book) |
| Odes Sol. | Odes of Solomon |
| Pesiq. Rab. | Pesiqta Rabbati |
| Pirqe. R. El. | Pirqe Rabbi Eliezer |
| Pss. Sol. | Psalms of Solomon |
| Rab. | Rabbah (+biblical book); (e.g., Gen. Rab.=Genesis Rabbah) |
| S. ʿOlam Rab. | Seder ʿOlam Rabbah |
| Sem. | Semahot |
| Sib. Or. | Sibylline Oracles |
| T. Ab. | Testament of Abraham |
| T. Adam | Testament of Adam |
| T. Ash. | Testament of Asher |
| T. Benj. | Testament of Benjamin |
| T. Dan | Testament of Dan |
| T. Gad | Testament of Gad |
| T. Hez. | Testament of Hezekiah |
| T. Isaac | Testament of Isaac |
| T. Iss. | Testament of Issachar |
| T. Jac. | Testament of Jacob |
| T. Job | Testament of Job |
| T. Jos. | Testament of Joseph |
| T. Jud. | Testament of Judah |
| T. Levi | Testament of Levi |
| T. Mos. | Testament of Moses |
| T. Naph. | Testament of Naphtali |
| T. Reu. | Testament of Reuben |
| T. Sim. | Testament of Simeon |
| T. Sol. | Testament of Solomon |
| T. Zeb. | Testament of Zebulum |
| Tanh. | Tanhuma |
| Tg. Isa. | Targum of Isaiah |
| Tg. Lam. | Targum of Lamentations |
| Tg. Neof. | Targum Neofiti |
| Tg. Onq. | Targum Onqelos |
| Tg. Ps.-J | Targum Pseudo-Jonathan |
| y. | Jerusalem Talmud (+ tractate) |

## 3. Classical Historians

For an extended list of classical historians and church fathers, see *SBL Handbook of Style*, pp. 84–87. For many works of classical antiquity, the abbreviations have been subjected to the author's discretion; the names of these works should be obvious upon consulting entries of the classical writers in classical dictionaries or encyclopedias.

### *Eusebius*

| | |
|---|---|
| Eccl. Hist. | Ecclesiastical History |

### *Josephus*

| | |
|---|---|
| Ag. Ap. | Against Apion |
| Ant. | Jewish Antiquities |
| J.W. | Jewish War |
| Life | The Life |

### *Philo*

| | |
|---|---|
| Abraham | On the Life of Abraham |
| Agriculture | On Agriculture |
| Alleg. Interp | Allegorical Interpretation |
| Animals | Whether Animals Have Reason |
| Cherubim | On the Cherubim |
| Confusion | On the Confusion of Thomas |
| Contempl. Life | On the Contemplative Life |
| Creation | On the Creation of the World |
| Curses | On Curses |
| Decalogue | On the Decalogue |
| Dreams | On Dreams |
| Drunkenness | On Drunkenness |
| Embassy | On the Embassy to Gaius |
| Eternity | On the Eternity of the World |
| Flaccus | Against Flaccus |
| Flight | On Flight and Finding |
| Giants | On Giants |
| God | On God |
| Heir | Who Is the Heir? |
| Hypothetica | Hypothetica |
| Joseph | On the Life of Joseph |
| Migration | On the Migration of Abraham |
| Moses | On the Life of Moses |
| Names | On the Change of Names |
| Person | That Every Good Person Is Free |
| Planting | On Planting |
| Posterity | On the Posterity of Cain |
| Prelim. Studies | On the Preliminary Studies |
| Providence | On Providence |
| QE | Questions and Answers on Exodus |
| QG | Questions and Answers on Genesis |
| Rewards | On Rewards and Punishments |
| Sacrifices | On the Sacrifices of Cain and Abel |
| Sobriety | On Sobriety |
| Spec. Laws | On the Special Laws |
| Unchangeable | That God Is Unchangeable |
| Virtues | On the Virtues |

| Worse | That the Worse Attacks the Better |
|---|---|

## Apostolic Fathers

| 1 Clem. | First Letter of Clement |
|---|---|
| Barn. | Epistle of Barnabas |
| Clem. Hom. | Ancient Homily of Clement (also called 2 Clement) |
| Did. | Didache |
| Herm. Vis.; Sim. | Shepherd of Hermas, Visions; Similitudes |
| Ignatius | Epistles of Ignatius (followed by the letter's name) |
| Mart. Pol. | Martyrdom of Polycarp |

## 4. Modern Abbreviations

| AASOR | Annual of the American Schools of Oriental Research |
|---|---|
| AB | Anchor Bible |
| ABD | Anchor Bible Dictionary |
| ABRL | Anchor Bible Reference Library |
| AGJU | Arbeiten zur Geschichte des antiken Judentums und des Urchristentums |
| AH | Agricultural History |
| ALGHJ | Arbeiten zur Literatur und Geschichte des Hellenistischen Judentums |
| AnBib | Analecta biblica |
| ANRW | Aufstieg und Niedergang der römischen Welt |
| ANTC | Abingdon New Testament Commentaries |
| BAGD | Bauer, W., W. F. Arndt, F. W. Gingrich, and F. W. Danker. Greek-English Lexicon of the New Testament and Other Early Christina Literature (2d. ed.) |
| BA | Biblical Archaeologist |
| BAFCS | Book of Acts in Its First Century Setting |
| BAR | Biblical Archaeology Review |
| BASOR | Bulletin of the American Schools of Oriental Research |
| BBC | Bible Background Commentary |
| BBR | Bulletin for Biblical Research |
| BDB | Brown, F., S. R. Driver, and C. A. Briggs. A Hebrew and English Lexicon of the Old Testament |
| BDF | Blass, F., A. Debrunner, and R. W. Funk. A Greek Grammar of the New Testament and Other Early Christian Literature |
| BECNT | Baker Exegetical Commentary on the New Testament |
| BI | Biblical Illustrator |
| Bib | Biblica |
| BibSac | Bibliotheca Sacra |

| BLT | Brethren Life and Thought |
|---|---|
| BNTC | Black's New Testament Commentary |
| BRev | Bible Review |
| BSHJ | Baltimore Studies in the History of Judaism |
| BST | The Bible Speaks Today |
| BSV | Biblical Social Values |
| BT | The Bible Translator |
| BTB | Biblical Theology Bulletin |
| BZ | Biblische Zeitschrift |
| CBQ | Catholic Biblical Quarterly |
| CBTJ | Calvary Baptist Theological Journal |
| CGTC | Cambridge Greek Testament Commentary |
| CH | Church History |
| CIL | Corpus inscriptionum latinarum |
| CPJ | Corpus papyrorum judaicorum |
| CRINT | Compendia rerum iudaicarum ad Novum Testamentum |
| CTJ | Calvin Theological Journal |
| CTM | Concordia Theological Monthly |
| CTT | Contours of Christian Theology |
| DBI | Dictionary of Biblical Imagery |
| DCM | Dictionary of Classical Mythology. |
| DDD | Dictionary of Deities and Demons in the Bible |
| DJBP | Dictionary of Judaism in the Biblical Period |
| DJG | Dictionary of Jesus and the Gospels |
| DLNT | Dictionary of the Later New Testament and Its Developments |
| DNTB | Dictionary of New Testament Background |
| DPL | Dictionary of Paul and His Letters |
| EBC | Expositor's Bible Commentary |
| EDBT | Evangelical Dictionary of Biblical Theology |
| EDNT | Exegetical Dictionary of the New Testament |
| EJR | Encyclopedia of the Jewish Religion |
| EPRO | Études préliminaires aux religions orientales dans l'empire romain |
| EvQ | Evangelical Quarterly |
| ExpTim | Expository Times |
| FRLANT | Forsuchungen zur Religion und Literatur des Alten und Neuen Testament |
| GNC | Good News Commentary |
| GNS | Good News Studies |
| HCNT | Hellenistic Commentary to the New Testament |
| HDB | Hastings Dictionary of the Bible |

# Zondervan Illustrated Bible Backgrounds Commentary

# MARK

by David E. Garland

## Authorship and Place of Origin

The writer of this Gospel wished only to give witness to Jesus Christ and not to identify himself, but ancient testimony has always attributed it to Mark. When the Gospels were shared with other communities, they needed titles so that hearers would know what was being read and readers would know what was on the shelf. Had they circulated anonymously, each community would have given them a different title. Why accredit a Gospel to someone not known as an apostle unless there was some basis for this in fact?

Ancient tradition also connects Mark to Peter. Some claim that this testimony is muddled, but the Gospel's relationship to Peter is likely. The author would certainly not have been an unknown upstart who decided independently to write a Gospel. He must have been a recognized teacher in the church who could appeal to an even greater authority — Peter. That Matthew and Luke allowed themselves to be guided by Mark in writing their Gospels testifies to this fact.

**AREA OF CAESAREA PHILIPPI**

The waterfall at Banias, near the source of the Jordan River.

◀

## ▶ Mark
## IMPORTANT FACTS:

- ■ **AUTHOR:** John Mark, coworker of the apostle Peter.
- ■ **DATE:** Between A.D. 68 and A.D. 70.
- ■ **OCCASION:** There was terrible social upheaval in Palestine and throughout the Mediterranean world for the Jews. Life was also difficult for the early Christians. It was a time of suffering and martyrdom.
- ■ **KEY THEMES:**
  1. To fortify the faith of believers who were suffering.
  2. To explain the current suffering of believers.
  3. To admonish "cross-bearing" as integral to discipleship.
  4. To encourage believers with hope — in spite of their failures.

Where Mark wrote his Gospel is difficult to decide. Tradition associates it with Rome, which may explain why Mark must interpret Palestinian customs for his audience (e.g., 7:3 – 5, washing of hands; 15:42, the "day of preparation" is the day before Sabbath).[1] A good case can also be made for the Palestinian origin of the Gospel, however.

## Setting and Purpose

Wherever this Gospel was written, it addressed a setting of persecution and crisis, probably around A.D. 68 – 70. The Roman historian, Tacitus, described the period of the late 60s this way:

The history on which I am entering is that of a period rich in disasters, terrible with battles, torn by civil struggles, horrible even in peace. Four emperors fell by the sword; there were three civil wars, more foreign wars, and often both at the same time. . . . Italy was distressed by disasters unknown before or returning after the lapse of the ages. . . . Beside the manifold misfortunes that befell mankind there were prodigies in the sky and on the earth, warnings given by thunderbolts, and prophecies of the future, both joyful and gloomy, uncertain and clear.[2]

Jews faced even greater catastrophes. When Mark wrote, a Roman legion either was on the verge of or had recently sacked Jerusalem and demolished the temple. The discourse in Mark 13 suggests that Christians faced the full brunt of Satan's onslaught. In addition to the social upheaval created by wars and the desecration of what was once a revered and holy shrine (13:7 – 8, 14), Christians had to deal with inquisitions (13:9), betrayal (13:12), family crack-ups (13:12), and hatred because of their faith (13:13). False prophets proliferated, peddling false hope (13:5 – 6).

In a context of suffering and martyrdom, Mark wrote:

(1) *To fortify the faith of those in danger of being overwhelmed by fear (4:41; 10:32; 16:8).* They may cry out in the midst of storms, "Don't you care if we drown?" (4:38). Mark seeks to lift the community's "eyes from the surging chaos that seems to engulf it and to fix them instead on the vision of the one enthroned in heaven, the monarch omnipotent in every storm."[3]

**THE TEMPLE MOUNT**

Leen Ritmeyer's classic reconstruction of the Jerusalem Temple.

▼

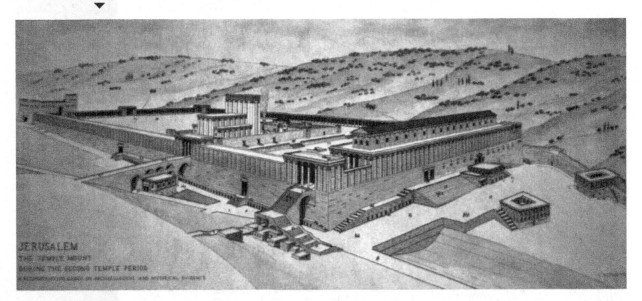

JERUSALEM
THE TEMPLE MOUNT
DURING THE SECOND TEMPLE PERIOD
A RECONSTRUCTION BASED ON ARCHAEOLOGICAL AND HISTORICAL EVIDENCE

**(2)** *To account for the present circumstances of believers.* Jesus promises his followers rewards but only with persecutions (10:29 – 30). He warns that they will be salted with fire (9:49 – 50). Their suffering is all part of the mystery of how the kingdom of God advances in the world.

**(3)** *To admonish.* Cross-bearing is not optional but an integral requirement of discipleship (8:34 – 38). The disciples' sad performance provides a negative example of those who prefer glory to arduous hardship. Having no root in themselves, they endure awhile but fall away when affliction arises because of the word (4:17). Jesus' behavior under severe trial sets the standard the community must follow.

**(4)** *To encourage.* Despite their grievous failures, Jesus never disowns his disciples and promises a renewed relationship after his resurrection (16:7). Readers would know, for example, that Peter repented, was restored, and died a martyr for the faith. They learn from Mark that God overcomes human weakness and that Jesus' death and resurrection atones for even the worst sins.

**(5)** *To prevent believers from being deluded by end-time delirium.* Mark wants to fit readers with spiritual lenses that will allow them to see clearly heavenly realities through the blinding cloudbursts of earthly disasters.

**(6)** *To fit Christ's followers for mission to all the world (14:9).* They are not selected for special privileges but sent out to call others to repent and believe the gospel (6:12). They are to feed spiritually hungry masses (6:37).

**(7)** *To inform pious interest in Jesus their Lord.* Mark gives a human face to the one whom these people believe is the Christ, the Son of God. Jesus is a real person firmly planted in the soil of everyday Palestinian life.

## Prologue (1:1 – 13)

Mark opens his Gospel with a prologue that provides the reader with privileged information unavailable to the characters in the story other than Jesus. A transcendent voice from offstage announces that John's ministry fulfills divine prophecy and then identifies Jesus as the beloved Son and the conveyor of the Spirit. Next, Mark shows Jesus confronting and defeating Satan, living at peace with the wild animals, and being served by angels.

**The beginning of the gospel about Jesus Christ (1:1).** "Gospel" refers to the story about Jesus narrated in the text, but it also includes the oral tradition that supplements the text. It comprises Jesus' words, deeds, death, and resurrection as God's direct intervention into history; it challenges an imperial cult propaganda that promotes a message of good tidings and a new age of peace through the Roman emperor.

This opening line may serve as the introduction to the opening segment of Mark (1:1 – 13) or may be the title Mark

JUDEA

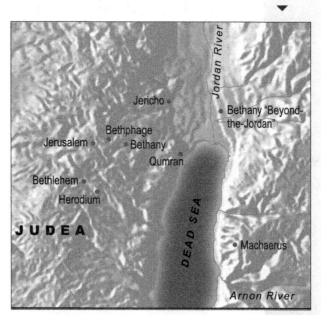

gives to his Gospel or the summary of its contents. If the latter, it explains why Mark abruptly ends the story with the women fleeing the tomb (16:8). The Gospel is open-ended. The reader knows that their flight and silence are not the end of the matter but is not given the details of how their fear was vanquished or their mouths opened. The end, therefore, serves as a beginning to a story to be continued (cf. Acts 1:1 – 2).

**The Son of God (1:1).** With the title "Son of God," Mark affirms that a profound relationship exists between Jesus and God, but this term's long history in the ancient Near East and the Old Testament meant it had a variety of associations. It would not necessarily have implied divinity or preexistence as it does for most today. The Old Testament applied the term to angelic figures[4] and to Israel as chosen and protected by God.[5] The expression was also used for the individual righteous Jew;[6] and in *Joseph and Asenath*, Joseph was called firstborn "son of God" because of his beauty.[7] Most relevant is God's declaration that the one who ascends the royal throne is "my son."[8] These enthronement passages invited the use of "son" as a title for the royal Messiah. Though it was only rarely employed in Palestinian Judaism, evidence exists for its usage as a messianic title in pre-Christian Judaism.[9] Clearly, the high priest's query, "Are you the Christ, the Son of the Blessed One?" (14:61), treats "Christ" and "Son of God" as equivalent.

The title had a variety of connotations in the Greco-Roman world. It was applied to figures such as Heracles, who shared the characteristics of a heroic mortal and of a god. The emperor Augustus received the title *divi filius*, the son of the deified one (Julius Caesar). The Roman emperors and members of their family were deified posthumously, while Gaius Caligula (and later Commodus) sought to emphasize his own divinity during his lifetime. The idea of bestowing divine honors and titles on human beings, however, was more accepted in the East, which was accustomed to ruler cults. An inscription on a stele in Pergamum identifies Augustus as "emperor Caesar, Son of God, God Augustus."[10] In this context, the expression would have been deemed fitting for a king or ruler as well as a divine figure (see Acts 14:11).

Mark's doubling of terms such as "Christ, the Son of God" serves as a two-step progression in which the second element has the effect of sharpening and heightening "the meaning of what precedes."[11] "Son of God" therefore means more than that Jesus is the Messiah or a royal ruler. Mark's narrative does not simply present Jesus as the long-awaited Messiah but as one who is God's Son in a unique way. The unclean spirits possess supernatural knowledge and recognize that Jesus is the Son of God who has come to destroy them (3:11; 5:7; see 1:24). They attest to his divine nature, authority, and power, not that he is Israel's Messiah. Mark also describes Jesus doing what only God can do. He battles Satan, calls disciples with the power of God, casts out demons, heals fever, cures leprosy, forgives sins, controls the sea, raises the dead, walks on the waves, and miraculously feeds thousands; and his death unleashes apocalyptic events. His coming signifies not the advent of some earthly messianic rule but the advent of the reign of God that will subjugate principalities and powers, things present and things to come, things above the earth and things beneath the earth, and even death.

**It is written in Isaiah the prophet (1:2).** The gospel message continues a longer story stretching back to Isaiah. Mark quotes from three texts: the law (Ex. 23:20 LXX), the greater prophets (Isa. 40:3), and the minor prophets (Mal. 3:1, the last of the prophets) to attest that God initiates the action.[12] Postbiblical Judaism tended to combine Old Testament texts in much the same way that modern hymnals conflate various texts in responsive readings. No simple device, such as footnotes, existed to identify all of the texts cited. By singling out Isaiah as the source, Mark informs the reader that the story "is to be understood against the backdrop of Isaian themes."[13]

**John came, baptizing in the desert region (1:4).** John chooses to preach and baptize in the desert for its symbolic associations. (1) For Israel, the desert was the place of new beginnings and renewal.[14] (2) It was also the place one went to elude persecution and to flee iniquity, since it was beyond the control of the cities.[15] According to the *Martyrdom of Isaiah* 2:7 – 11, the prophets Isaiah, Micah, Ananias, Joel, Habbakuk, and Josab, his son, abandoned the corruption of Judah for the desert. They clothed themselves in sackcloth, lamented straying Israel, and ate wild herbs as an act of symbolic judgment. The covenanters at Qumran cited Isaiah 40:3 as warrant for separating themselves from sinners "to walk to the desert in order to open there His path."[16] (3) The desert was also viewed as the mobilizing area for God's future victory over evil and the place where Elijah (Mal. 4:5) and the Messiah were thought to appear (Matt. 24:26). On the other side of the Jordan (John 1:28), John draws the people away from Jerusalem to the place where Israel had once stood prior to entering the Promised Land.

**A baptism of repentance for the forgiveness of sins (1:4).** John demands that everyone who comes for his baptism seal his or her pledge of repentance. A Jewish tradition claimed that Israel was prepared on Sinai for receiving salvation by means of immersion.[17] According to the prophets, Israel's cleansing was preparation for receiving God's Spirit.[18]

Ritual immersion was a common practice in Judaism, so common that the wealthier inhabitants of Jerusalem had their own immersion pools built in their houses. Nearly 150 of them have been found. Immersion pools had to contain

**THE JUDEAN WIL-DERNESS**

*(left)* Jebel Qurun-tul, a mountain in the desert near Jericho associated with the tempta-tion of Jesus.

*(right)* The mon-astery of the Mount of Temptation.

▼

forty seahs of water (a *seah* equals a little less than two gallons). They were to be one cubit square and three cubits deep to enable people standing in it to immerse themselves completely by bending their knees.[19] This standard Jewish practice probably means that John did not immerse each person but served as the priestly mediator supervising the people as they submerged themselves by bending forward into the water.

John's baptism differs significantly from normal Jewish immersions for ceremonial purification because it is done only once and does not need repeating. It is not simply a rite of cleansing but an initiatory rite in which the one baptized repents and accepts God's offer of forgiveness to be saved from the coming fiery judgment. Josephus's description of John's baptism as only a purificatory rite and his statement that "they must not employ it to gain pardon for whatever sins they committed" suggests that he found this idea offensive.[20]

**John wore clothing made of camel's hair, with a leather belt around his waist (1:6).** John's clothing conjures up images of the prophet Elijah, who wore the same things.[21] According to 2 Kings 2:5 – 14, Elijah was taken up on the banks of the Jordan near Jericho. John may have deliberately chosen this site for his baptism because of its associations with Elijah and with Elisha's request for a double share of his spirit.

**And he ate locusts and wild honey (1:6).** The diet conveys asceticism and piety. Locusts were ritually clean and therefore permitted for Jews to eat (Lev. 11:20 – 23). They could "be cooked in salt-water, or roasted on coals, then dried, reduced to powder, and eaten with

salt."[22] Josephus also refers to an abundance of bees in this region that would have produced ample honey.[23]

**The thongs of whose sandals I am not worthy to stoop down and untie (1:7).** John preaches that a more powerful person is coming who will baptize with the Spirit. The "strong one" is a name for God in the Greek Old Testament (LXX). John's water baptism is only preparatory as people plunge into the Jordan, signifying their repentance to ready themselves for God's coming kingdom. The Spirit's baptism will be definitive. John comes as a voice crying, a servant unworthy to perform even the demeaning task of stooping to loosen the sandals of the one who comes after him. A rabbinic commentary takes Leviticus 25:39, "do not make him work as a slave" to mean:

A Hebrew slave must not wash the feet of his master, nor put his shoes on him, nor carry his things before him when going to the bathhouse, nor support him by the hips when ascending steps, nor carry him in a litter or a sedan chair as slaves do. For it is said: "But over your brethren the children of Israel ye shall not rule, over one another, with rigor" (Lev. 25:46).[24]

**He saw heaven being torn open (1:10).** The heavens are usually described as "opening" as a sign that God is about to speak or act.[25] Mark says they are "torn" at Jesus' baptism, just as the temple veil is "torn" at his death (15:38). Joshua (Josh. 3:14 – 17), Elijah (2 Kings 2:8), and Elisha (2:14) each parted the Jordan river, and the false prophet Theudas promised to do it.[26] By contrast, when Jesus is baptized in the Jordan, the heavens are parted, recalling the longing expressed in Isaiah 64:1, "Oh, that you would rend the heavens and come down, that the mountains would tremble before you!"

**The Spirit descending on him like a dove (1:10).** This detail recalls the image of the Spirit's hovering over the waters at the beginning of creation (Gen. 1:2), as well as a rabbinic tradition that describes the Spirit's hovering like a dove.[27] God's Spirit swooping down on Jesus signifies the beginning of a new creation. The image confirms that Jesus' ministry will be Spirit directed (Isa. 11:2).

The rabbis relegated the Spirit's activity to the past because their authority was based on their ability to interpret previous revelation. To protect that authority, they undermined any who acted unconventionally and claimed more direct links to the divine through the Spirit.[28] A rabbinic tradition says that the Holy Spirit came to an end in Israel when the last prophets (Haggai, Zechariah, and Malachi) died. From then on, one could only hear the heavenly messages from an echo, the daughter of the voice (*bat qôl*). It continues that the sages were gathered in an upper room when the heavenly voice said, "There is a man among you who is worthy to receive the Holy Spirit, but his generation is unworthy of such an honor." They assumed that the person was Hillel the elder.[29] Significantly, Mark begins his gospel by featuring the work of the prophet John the Baptizer and the descent of the Spirit on Jesus. The Spirit has not come to an end in Israel but is breaking loose in a new, momentous way.

**The Spirit sent him out into the desert (1:12).** The Spirit does not induce a state of inner tranquility but drives Jesus deeper into the desolate desert, where wild beasts prowl, and into the clutches of Satan. The desert was also known as God's proving grounds for the people. Jesus emerges victorious over Satan, and his healing ministry continues his onslaught on Satan's realm.

---

## ▶ The Kingdom of God

The kingdom of God is not primarily a spatial or temporal category but refers to God's active reign. God approaches with strength (Isa. 40:10 LXX) to establish "his dominion over sin, sickness and hostile powers." In the ancient world, kingship conveyed power, sovereignty, dominion, and preeminence; but in the Old Testament kingship was also connected to ruling with justice and mercy. For Israel, God alone was King, who ruled over all creation, powers, and peoples.[A-1] In this period of oppression under pagan rulers, many pious Jews expected God to establish a transcendental kingdom greater than all the kingdoms of earth and to avenge injustice, destroy the wicked, and vanquish the host of Satan. God's reign claimed the people's absolute obedience. They must sever all other allegiances and completely submit to God's law.

For zealous militants, the rallying cry "God is King" became a call to arms and fierce resistance to the pagan encroachment in God's land. For the sect at Qumran, it meant withdrawing into the desert to await the final battle between God's angelic army and the forces of evil. For the Pharisees, it meant intensifying obedience to strict interpretations of the law, what they called building a fence around the law, to establish and preserve the holiness of the people in preparation.[A-2] For Jesus, the kingdom of God denotes something quite different. It signals a divine outbreak of mercy and forgiveness, of healing and restoration. It entails good news to the oppressed, the sick, the demon-possessed, the impure, and moral outcasts. Jesus' preaching challenges nationalistic expectations and ritual protocol.

## Beginning of Jesus' Ministry (1:14 – 15)

**After John was put in prison (1:14).** The announcement that John was "delivered up" (the literal meaning of "put in prison") foreshadows how the fates of John and Jesus will be intertwined. Jesus also will be delivered up.[30] John is Jesus' forerunner in ministry, conflict with earthly authorities, and death (6:7 – 13; 9:11 – 13).

**Jesus went into Galilee, proclaiming the good news of God. "The time has come," he said. "The kingdom of God is near" (1:14 – 15).** With the forerunner's work completed, Jesus' work now begins as he returns victoriously from his battle with Satan. He announces God's timely intervention into the present. The time of waiting is over, and the decisive moment has arrived when God's rule will be established.[31]

## Calling of the First Disciples (1:16 – 20)

**Simon and his brother Andrew casting a net into the lake (1:16).** Jesus calls Peter and Andrew as they are casting nets from the shoreline. Early church tradition suggests that this scene took place in the cove of Tabgha, west of Capernaum. Warm mineral springs flowed into the lake there, attracting schools of fish.[32] We should not presume that they were too poor to own a boat. In the winter, a type of fish called *musht* "move closer to the shore in schools to seek warmer waters." One expert notes that "twentieth-century fisherman continue to use this spring, now known as Ein Nur, for these purposes."[33] The throw net was eighteen to twenty-five feet in diameter, with a rope in its center and lead sinkers on its circumference. It was cast by one person standing in a boat or on a rock near the lakeshore. The net was laid on one arm and shoulder and was then thrown with a large swing of the other arm. The net sank to the bottom like an opened parachute capturing the fish. The fisherman then had to pull out the fish one by one or carefully draw all the lead weights together and haul the catch to shore or into a boat.

**"Come, follow me" (1:17).** Jesus' first act creates a community of followers by calling some to follow him. Prophets did not call people to follow them, but to follow God. The teachers of the law had disciples who came to them to be instructed in the law, but none ever said to anyone, "Come, follow me." The disciple, rather, always chose the master and moved on when he believed that he had learned as much from him as possible about the tradition. Jesus does not wait for volunteers but chooses his own disciples and requires absolute obedience. Mark shows Jesus calling disciples with divine authority, just as God called the prophets in the Old Testament and expected the relationship to be permanent. He also does not call them to a house of study but to an itinerant ministry.

**I will make you fishers of men (1:17).** In the Old Testament, the metaphor of fishing for men is associated with gathering people for judgment.[34] For Jesus, the imagery has to do with a messianic gathering of the people. In *Joseph and Asenath*, Joseph's new wife prays a psalm of thanksgiving after her conversion and says that her husband "grasped me like a fish on a hook."[35] The disciples are called to be agents who will bring a compelling message to others, one that will change their lives beyond recognition.

He saw James son of Zebedee and his brother John in a boat, preparing their nets (1:19). After each outing, fishing nets required mending, washing, drying, and folding, and Jesus finds John and James engaged in this task. Three types of nets were used in New Testament times: the seine net (Matt. 13:47 – 48), the cast net (Mark 1:16), and the trammel net, which could stretch to five hundred feet and required two boats working together. Owning a boat does not indicate that Zebedee and his sons are well-to-do, any more than owning a yoke of oxen or a flock of sheep indicates that a farmer is well-to-do. Note how both the boat owner and the hired laborers are pictured working side by side. Fish suppliers had to lease their fishing rights, and these fishermen are probably part of a fishing cooperative that has contracted to deliver fish to wealthier middlemen.

## The Man with an Unclean Spirit (1:21 – 28)

When the Sabbath came, Jesus went into the synagogue and began to teach (1:21). The remains of a limestone synagogue visible today in Capernaum date from the late second to third century or perhaps as late as the fifth century. Religious structures were normally rebuilt in the same sacred area, and an earlier building made of rough black basalt stones has been discovered beneath it. It is probable that the synagogue in Jesus' day was located in the same spot, and its outline fits the plan of early synagogues found at Masada, Herodium, Gamla, and

## ▶ Capernaum

The village of Capernaum (*Kefar Nahum* in Hebrew) was located on the northwest shore of the Sea of Galilee, two miles west of the upper Jordan River, some 680 feet below sea level. It was the first town west of the border between the tetrarchy assigned to Herod Antipas and that assigned to Herod Philip (Gaulanitus) and sat east of the extension of the Via Maris highway to Damascus. The village's situation on this frontier gave it some importance. It had a customs office manned by Levi (Mark 2:13 – 15) and a detachment of soldiers under a centurion (Luke 7:1 – 10; Matt. 8:5 – 13). By the time of Josephus, however, it had apparently lost its significance. Josephus claimed to have organized the defense in Galilee in the war against Rome but gave Capernaum only incidental mention as the place where he fell off a horse and as a fertile district for grapes and figs with a "genial air" and watered by "a highly fertilizing spring."[A-3]

Capernaum's economy was based on fishing, agriculture, industry (manufacture of tools made from basalt stones and of glass vessels), and trade. This side of the lake was particularly rich for fishing, which may explain why Peter and his brother Andrew left their hometown Bethsaida and settled here. The coins and vessels uncovered by archaeologists suggest that the village was commercially linked to the northern regions of upper Galilee, Golan, Syria, Phoenicia, Asia Minor, and Cyprus.

Archaeologists estimate the population of the town to have been between 1,000 to 1,500. The private houses that have been excavated are unpretentious and average for the living standard of an ancient village. Local volcanic basalt stones in their natural state were used to build walls and pavements. The houses had a single door opening onto a public street and consisted of several roofed rooms clustered around a large open courtyard that served as the focal point where daily activities such as cooking and craft work took place. Houses of this kind were probably shared by two or more kindred families governed by a patriarchal structure.

Magdala. It measures 4,838 square feet and is the largest of the synagogues found from this era.[36]

The Palestinian synagogues dating from the third and fourth centuries with their external and internal ornamentation, Torah niches, and raised platforms may mislead us to expect first-century synagogues to look much the same. By contrast, the synagogues of the first century "were functional and plain."[37] Synagogues became more official institutions in the second and third centuries after the temple's destruction created a desire to create an organization for nonsacrificial worship.[38]

**A man . . . possessed by an evil spirit (1:23).** Mark uses the term "unclean [*akatharton*] spirit" rather than "evil [*poneron*] spirit." This is not a medical diagnosis, but a religious term. In the Old Testament, that which is unclean has evaded the control of the divine holiness and causes humans to be banished from God's presence.[39] Jesus, endued with the Holy Spirit, has come to purify what is unclean.

Mark draws a distinction between those who are demonized and those who

are sick (1:32, 34). Unlike the sick, those identified as controlled by demons have extraordinary strength (5:4) and suffer violently (5:5; 9:22). The demons, agitated by Jesus' presence, usually howl their alarm (1:24; 5:7) and often do some kind of harm when they depart. The possession is caused by an evil power that requires a greater power to expel it.

**"I know who you are — the Holy One of God!" (1:24).** The unclean spirit assumes that knowledge is power and tries to fend off its impending defeat with the exorcist's trick of pronouncing the name of the opponent. In the ancient magical papyri, names were used as incantations because it was believed that pronouncing the name of the power or enemy gave one a tactical advantage in manipulating and defeating it. The cry (lit.) "What between you and me?" (1:24) is the same cry used by the widow of Zarephath (1 Kings 17:18) and the king of the Ammonites (Judg. 11:12) as a defensive maneuver. A magical papyri drawn up to ward off demons illustrates the strategy: "I know your name which was received in heaven, I know your forms. . . . I know your foreign names and your true name. . . .

**CAPERNAUM**

*(left)* Remains of basalt homes. The modern structure in the background is built over the top of the site identified as the home of Peter.

*(right)* Remains of the home of Peter in Capernaum. The property was converted into a church during the 2d – 4th centuries A.D.

▼

I know you Hermes, who you are and whence you came."[40]

Unlike other exorcisms recorded in the ancient world, Jesus uses no incantations, chants, rites, noises, pharmaceutical recipes, knots, or other magical devices. In Tobit 8:2 – 3, for example, Sarah drives off the demon Asmodeus with the help of the angel Raphael by burning a fish's liver and heart, whose stench "repelled the demon . . . to the remotest parts of Egypt." Jesus makes no appeals to a supernatural power and does not rattle off a litany of powerful names. He simply commands, and the demons flee.

## Healing Peter's Mother-in-Law (1:29 – 34)

**They went . . . to the home of Simon and Andrew (1:29).** Archaeologists have uncovered a house that may well have been Peter's home. Inside the building, numerous coins, pottery, and oil lamps dating to the first century have been discovered, along with artifacts that include several fish hooks. It is located only one hundred feet south of the city's synagogue on the main street of the town and consists of a large, circular cluster of rooms around a spacious courtyard. An open area between the street and the doorway leading to the courtyard would have allowed space for a large number of people to "gather at the door" (1:33; cf. 2:1 – 3).

This site was venerated by later Christians from the inscriptions and symbols found in the debris. In the late first century, it was changed into a house for religious gatherings; and in the fourth century, it was enlarged and set apart from

▶ ## The Synagogue

Synagogues could be found everywhere in this era, but we should not always envision a distinctive building.[A-4] They were primarily gatherings of people, not buildings. In Jesus' time, most village synagogues were probably modified rooms in private homes or public buildings. Josephus describes the impetus for such gatherings:

> He [Moses] appointed the Law to be the most excellent and necessary form of instruction, ordaining, not that it should be heard once for all or twice or on several occasions, but that every week men should desert their other occupations and assemble to listen to the Law and to obtain a thorough and accurate knowledge of it, a practice which all other legislators seem to have neglected.[A-5]

A synagogue inscription found in Jerusalem on Mount Ophel illumines the synagogue's purpose as the place where the law was read and heard, taught and learned, interpreted and applied to life:

Theodotus [son of] Vettenus, priest and archisynagogos, son of the archisynagogos and grandson of the archisynagogos constructed the synagogue for the reading of the Law and the study of the commandments and the guest-room and the (upper?) chambers and the installations of the water for a hostelry for those needing [them] from abroad, which was founded by his fathers and the elders and Simonides.[A-6]

Philo gives us a picture of a group gathered around the study of the law. He describes an Egyptian in Alexandria arguing with Jews to break with their Sabbath customs: "And will you sit in your conventicles [synagogues] and assemble your regular company and read in security your holy books, expounding any obscure point and in leisurely comfort discussing at length your ancestral philosophy?"[A-7]

the rest of the town through an imposing enclosure wall. The pilgrim Egeria (ca. 383 – 95) wrote that "the house of the chief of the apostles has been turned into a church." In the second half of the fifth century, an octagonal church was built over the large room, probably to serve pilgrims, and remained in use until the seventh century, when Capernaum was conquered and destroyed by invading Muslim forces.

**Simon's mother-in-law (1:30).** When a woman married, she left her family and moved to the home and family of her husband. For this reason, daughters were not prized because they could not add to the family's wealth or honor. They were destined to become part of another's family, and a wife's blood relatives were not counted as kin by her new family. A mother-in-law would normally be living in her husband's house or, if he has died, in the home of a son. If she had no living sons, she would seek to return to her family. Otherwise, she would be destitute. Since Peter's mother-in-law has apparently moved to the home of her daughter, she has no living sons, and Peter has consented to accept responsibility for her. Another possibility, however, is that the home belongs to Peter's mother-in-law. Peter is said to come from Bethsaida (John 1:44), a few miles away; and he may have been visiting his mother-in-law.

An interesting ruling in the Mishnah insists that a man must tithe again any food that he gives his mother-in-law to prepare when he receives it back. It assumes that she will naturally want to exchange the produce given to her for something of better quality out of concern to improve the welfare of her daughter.[41]

**In bed with a fever (1:30).** A large segment of the ancient world considered fever to be an illness in and of itself caused by demons, divine beings, curses, or astrological phenomena.[42] In Leviticus 26:16 and Deuteronomy 28:22, fever is a divine chastisement. Many believed that it could only be cured by God. A rabbinic tradition reads: "Greater is the miracle wrought for the sick than for Hananiah, Mishael and Azariah. [For] that of Hananiah, Mishael and Azariah [concerned] a fire kindled by man, which all can extinguish; whilst that of a sick person is [in connection with] a heavenly fire, and who can extinguish that?"[43] The answer is that none can extinguish it except God. It is therefore Christologically significant that Jesus can extinguish a heavenly fire — something only God or God's agent could do.

**She began to wait on them (1:31).** Being able to serve others was a sign of physical and mental wholeness; it was not demeaning. "To wait on them" is the same verb ("to serve") used to describe what the angels did for Jesus in 1:13. It is also a characteristic of discipleship as Jesus makes clear to his disciples (9:35; 10:41 – 45). The women who saw his death from afar are described as those who "in Galilee . . . followed him and cared for his needs" (15:41).

## Prayer in a Lonely Place Before Going Out to the Whole of Galilee (1:35 – 39)

**Jesus . . . went off to a solitary place, where he prayed (1:35).** According to an ancient tradition, the "lonely place" was on the "ridge of hills" west of the village overlooking Tabgha and the Sea of Galilee.[44]

## Healing a Leper (1:39 – 41)

**A man with leprosy came to him (1:40).** In the New Testament, leprosy does not refer to Hansen's disease but to various

*right* ▶

**WATTLE AND
MUD ROOF**

Reconstruction
of the roof of a
typical rural home.

has been cleansed of his disease, he remains in social limbo until he has been examined and declared clean by a priest and has offered the appropriate sacrifices (see Lev. 14:1 – 32). The "testimony to them" may refer to the proof to the community into which the leper is being restored.

## Healing of a Paralytic (2:1 – 12)

**They made an opening in the roof above Jesus (2:4).** Houses in Capernaum did not have large windows. Walls were built without true foundations and were made of rough basalt without mortar. The courses were leveled with small pebbles and soil. Such buildings could support little more than a thatch roof. The sloping flat roof consisted of wooden cross beams (usually made from trees, Isa. 9:10) overlaid with a matting of reeds, palm branches, and dried mud (see Ps. 129:6). The roof could be reached from open courtyards by a flight of stone steps or by a ladder. One could then dig into the earthen roof without causing irreparable damage. This explains why the men could dig through the roof without evoking howls of protest from the owner. The roof had to be replenished and rolled every fall before the onset of the winter rains.

**GALILEE**

Capernaum was
located on the
north shore of the
Sea of Galilee.

▼

**The mat the paralyzed man was lying on (2:4).** Mark uses a colloquial word for a poor man's mat (see John 5:8). The pallet was probably a "cheap mattress, like a bag filled with straw."[53] When the bystanders glorify God in response to this miracle, it confirms that Jesus is not guilty of blasphemy.

**Son, your sins are forgiven (2:5).** Readers might find it surprising that Jesus first announces that the man's sins are forgiven rather than healing him. The men bring him to Jesus for healing, not absolution. Moderns tend to dissociate sin and our relationship to God from our physical well-being. In Jesus' world, people took for granted a connection between sickness and sins (see John 5:14; 9:2). Healing appears in conjunction with forgiveness in 2 Chronicles 7:14 and Psalm 103:3. Most assumed that reconciliation with God must occur before healing could come. In the Prayer of Nabonidus, found at Qumran, the king of Babylon says, "I was smitten [by a malignant inflammation] for seven years, and banished far [from men, until I prayed to the God Most High] and an exorcist forgave my sins. He was a Je[w] from [the exiles]."[54] In the Talmud, we find a tradition that "a sick man does not recover from his sickness

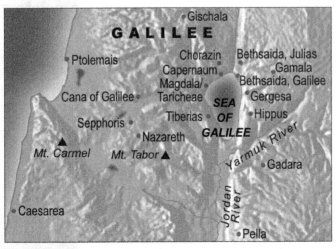

GALILEE

Gischala

Ptolemais
Chorazin  Bethsaida, Julias
Capernaum  Gamala
Magdala/  Bethsaida, Galilee
Cana of Galilee  Taricheae  SEA  Gergesa
Tiberias  OF  Hippus
Sepphoris  GALILEE
Nazareth  Yarmuk River
Mt. Carmel  Mt. Tabor ▲
Gadara
Jordan River
Caesarea
Pella

until all his sins are forgiven him, as it is written, 'Who forgiveth all thine iniquities, who healeth all thy diseases" (Ps. 103:3).' "[55] In another place, the rabbis appealed to Psalm 103:3 – 4 to explain why the prayer for forgiveness precedes the prayer for healing: "Redemption and healing come after forgiveness."[56]

A Jewish audience would surmise that the paralysis was a consequence of some sin.[57] To forgive the sin removes the consequences of the sin — the paralysis. The man's healing is therefore the result of the forgiveness of sins. The miracle shows that the coming of God's reign brings both forgiveness and healing.[58]

**He's blaspheming! Who can forgive sins but God alone? (2:7).** Jesus assumes the authority to remit sins as if he were God, even though he uses the divine passive, "Your sins are forgiven."[59] The teachers of the law conclude that Jesus blasphemously usurps God's prerogatives and affronts God's majesty, since only a priest could legitimately pronounce the forgiveness of sins on the basis of repentance, restitution, and sacrifice (Lev. 4; 5; 16; 17:11). Their hostile response unveils three things: (1) They admit that Jesus does something that they are unable to do — forgive sins. Their judgment confirms the crowd's earlier acclamation that Jesus teaches with new authority. (2) Blasphemy is a serious charge that emerges again during Jesus' trial (Mark 14:64). The text from Leviticus 24:16, that whoever "blasphemes the Name . . . must be put to death," cannot be far from their minds. The rejection of Jesus' authority to announce the forgiveness of sins will ultimately lead to his suffering and death for the forgiveness of sins. (3) Jesus knows hidden thoughts even as God does.[60] In *Joseph and Asenath* 23:8 and 26:6, prophets are said to perceive all things in their spirits (see Luke 7:39).

**Which is easier: to say to the paralytic, "Your sins are forgiven," or to say, "Get up, and take your mat and walk?" (2:9).** The alarm of these teachers of the law

---

▶ ## Scribes/Teachers of the Law

During the intertestamental period, the temple sacrificial cult was supplemented (not supplanted) by prayer and the study of the law in the synagogue. It was a lay institution that did not require the presence of a priest. As a result, the power of the priest became somewhat diluted by the learned scholar (teacher of the law or scribe). Unlike priests, scribes were not dependent on a special pedigree or institutional setting to function. Unlike prophets, they did not depend on direct contact with God or a charismatic personality. Judaism had become a book religion, and the scribe had authority on the basis of his erudition in sacred Scriptures and traditions. This does not exclude the possibility that scribes could be priests or Levites.

The hymn to the scribe in Sirach 38:24 – 39:11 presents the scribe as the ideal learned Jew. As interpreters of the law, they were regarded as custodians of the traditions on Jewish life and consulted by those in power (see Matt. 2:4). Some scribes were prominent advisors in the royal courts and leaders in the temple; others were lowly community officials or village copyists. Some were also visionaries.[A-8]

In Mark, the teachers of the law form a unified front in opposition to Jesus. His growing influence with the people imperils their importance. They appear alone (1:22; 2:6; 3:22; 9:11, 14; 12:28, 38), with the Pharisees (2:16; 7:5), and with the elders and chief priests (8:31; 11:27; 14:43, 53; 15:1).

is legitimate, and Jesus takes it seriously. At this stage of his ministry, Jesus is willing to give doubting teachers proof. He parries their indictment with a riddle that confirms his claim to divine authority. Moses offered a criterion to verify whether someone is a true or a false prophet who presumes to utter in God's name what the Lord has not uttered: "If what a prophet proclaims in the name of the LORD does not take place or come true, that is a message the LORD has not spoken. That prophet has spoken presumptuously. Do not be afraid of him" (Deut. 18:22).

Jesus' statement does not mean that one thing is easier than the other but that the two are interconnected. If the paralytic leaves on his own power, it will reveal that his sins have been forgiven, resulting in his complete healing.

### The Call of Levi the Tax Collector and Eating with Sinners (2:13 – 17)

**He saw Levi son of Alphaeus sitting at the tax collector's booth (2:14).** Since Levi is stationed in Galilee, he is most likely in the employ of Herod Antipas, a client king of Rome. The custom house is located near the border with Gaulanitus, under Herod Philip's rule, to collect tolls, tariffs, imposts, and customs on those goods entering and leaving the district or being transported through it. Levi also may have collected taxes from the fishing industry.

Toll collectors were renowned for dishonesty and extortion. Most pious Jews disdained them as desiring money more than honor or righteousness. They had sold out to a hostile culture. This would be particularly true for someone named Levi, assuming it was a typical name for Levites. In the *Testament of Levi* 13:1 – 2, Levi commands that his descendants learn to read and write so that they may read and understand the law. Levi's literacy may have opened up a quite different career path as an agent of an impious tetrarch.

Ironically, the rabbis sanctioned lying to a tax collector — except if one uses an oath, according to the School of Shammai, and even if one uses an oath, according to the School of Hillel.[61] Toll collectors were also detested throughout the Greco-Roman world. Plutarch wrote, "We are

### ▶ The Son of Man

No consensus exists about what this title (if it can be considered a title) was intended to conjure up in the minds of Jews in the first century. It appears thirteen times in Mark and only on the lips of Jesus. Was it supposed to evoke images of an apocalyptic heavenly figure, to punctuate his humanity (Ps. 8:4; 80:17; Ezek. 2:1), or simply to be understood as a circumlocution meaning "a man such as I"?[A-9]

When Jesus asked his disciples, "Who do people say I am?" "the Son of Man" was not one of the options cited (Mark 8:27 – 28). The obscurity of the term made it nearly free of any preconceived notions that Jesus' generation might entertain. It therefore was a mysterious and arresting title that Jesus could fill with his own meaning. In Mark, we do not get information about what the Son of Man is but what he does. He has authority to forgive sins (2:10) and is Lord of the Sabbath (2:28). He will be betrayed (14:21, 41), delivered up, suffer many things, die, and be raised (8:31, 38; 9:9, 12; 10:33). He came not to be served but to give his life as a ransom for many (10:45). He will come on the clouds (13:26) and will be seated at the right hand of power (14:62).

annoyed and displeased with customs-officials, not when they pick up those articles which we are importing openly, but when in the search for concealed goods they pry into baggage and merchandise which are another's property. And yet the law allows them to do this and they would lose by not doing so."[62] We should note, however, that Josephus cites John, the tax collector of Caesarea, as one of the leading Jews in the city, who took great risks in defending the sanctity of a synagogue.[63]

**Many tax collectors and "sinners" were eating with him and his disciples (2:15).** A celebratory meal was customary after conversion.[64]

One normally ate with one's relatives or with equals who would reciprocate. Jesus ate with toll collectors and sinners, that is, notorious sinners who had no intention of trying to conform to the demands of the law and became religious outcasts. By doing so, he made concrete God's offer of acceptance and forgiveness. Meals char-

◀ center

**SILVER COIN**

This coin depicts Tiberius, the Roman emperor during the ministry of Jesus (A.D. 14 – 37).

## ▶ Pharisees

The Pharisees were collections of lay factions unified by their concern for rigorous obedience to the law. They believed that only the worship and obedience of a holy people could preserve the land of Israel from judgment. Most Pharisees were not priests, but they sought to extend the concerns of ritual purity usually associated with priests in the temple into the lives of ordinary Jews outside the temple. They were especially known for their attention to purity rules that organized and classified things, times, and persons. The name means the "separated ones," and it was essential to their sense of "separateness" (holiness) to know what was permissible or proscribed, clean or unclean.

Pharisaic purity rules specified not only what might be eaten but out of which vessel and with whom one might eat. The Pharisees were particularly anxious that foodstuffs be properly grown, tithed, and prepared. They shunned contact with people that they labeled "the people of the land," who were less

conscientious about such things. The Pharisees regarded their table as an altar before God, and they sought to replicate the purity of the priests in the temple. Eating for them became a holy occasion.

In our culture, when we give a dinner party, we may worry about several things. Where will we eat — in the formal dining room or in the kitchen? Who sits where? Will the presence of a certain guest offend another guest? What should we serve? How do we prepare the food? What dinnerware do we use? What conversation is appropriate? What dress is appropriate? Guests at formal dinners may worry about which utensil to use with which course and may fear committing some gaffe. To the Pharisees, such questions had religious meaning. They gathered in hallowed groups to eat together in purity and reduce the risk of any pollution from the non-observant. The Pharisees believed that sinners should be kept at arm's length until decontaminated by proper repentance and the ceremonial rites.

acterize Jesus' ministry and have a distinctive character. (1) They are spontaneous affairs not tied to the cycle of holy times (e.g., Passover), nor are they an expression of a strictly regimented communal pattern (e.g., Qumran). (2) They represent the joyous celebration of God's saving reign bursting into the lives of people. (3) By being open to all, Jesus shows no fear that he will be tainted by the impurity or iniquity of sinners. On the contrary, he will infect them with the grace of God.

Sharing a table with others was a sign of friendship and goodwill. In not being choosy about his eating companions, Jesus ignores purity boundaries and provokes the Pharisees' ire.[65] He torpedoes the whole system of ranking and classifying people where the devout are to be extolled and sinners shunned. Jesus accepts into his fellowship social outcasts and sinners forgiven by grace.

**When the teachers of the law who were Pharisees saw him eating (2:16).** "The teachers of the law who were Pharisees" reads literally "the scribes of the Pharisees." As laymen, most Pharisees were not learned scholars. The "scribes of the Pharisees" were those in the movement who had more formal study and had become expert guides in the law. These teachers laid out clear guidelines and boundaries for what was acceptable and unacceptable to God in all spheres of life.

Feasting was usually in the open, and people were attracted by the noise of conversation and the smell of food. The pious Pharisees, who so exalted the sacredness of meals, fume over Jesus' public behavior. He violates instructions laid down throughout Scripture not to associate with evildoers.[66] A later rabbinic tradition attributes to the wise this extreme saying, "Let not a man associate with sinners even to bring them near to the Torah."[67]

**It is not the healthy who need a doctor, but the sick (2:17).** The proverbial wisdom about physicians can be found in Hellenistic circles, where it notes the duty and habit of physicians to be with the diseased. Jesus uses the proverb to emphasize "the need of the sick to have a physician."[68] Jesus embodies God's mercy and purpose to take away the diseases, infirmities, and sins of the people.

## The Question of Fasting (2:18 – 22)

**How is it that John's disciples and the disciples of the Pharisees are fasting, but yours are not? (2:18).** The Day of Atonement was the only time when God's law prescribed that the people were to deny themselves food.[69] The more ascetic disciples of John and the conscientious Pharisees fasted more often (see Luke 18:12). Observers, noting that Jesus' disciples do not fast, ask why.

Fasting was associated with three things: (1) sorrow for a deceased person; (2) penitential mourning to mollify the wrath of God and to avert calamity; and (3) petition to God.[70] According to the *Psalms of Solomon* 3:6 – 8, the righteous one avoids repeated sins, "searches his house to remove unintentional sins," and "atones for (sins of) ignorance by fasting and humbling his soul, and the Lord will cleanse every devout person and his house." Fasting could also be related to a fear of demons, who were thought to gain power over someone through eating.

**How can the guests of the bridegroom fast while he is with them (2:19).** Jesus explains his unwillingness to fast with a wedding analogy. Weddings were marked by music, laughter, feasting, and merrymaking. Anyone fasting at a wedding called attention to oneself and would be a grievous affront to the host. Jesus' rejection of fasting here is related to the joy, celebration, and hope that the presence of God's kingdom should excite. The Old Testament uses the image of the bridegroom for God, but clearly the image applies here to Jesus, who will be taken from them — the first allusion to his death in this Gospel.[71]

**A patch . . . wineskins (2:21 – 22).** The images of patching cloth and wineskins draw on everyday wisdom. The new stronger fabric of a patch will tear away from the old, weaker fabric when the garment is washed. Old wineskins already stretched to their limits will burst their seams when the new wine continues to ferment and emit gas. Combining new with old will result in torn garments, spilled wine, and ruined wineskins. The point is that the old — the old forms of Judaism — is incompatible with the new, not because the old is outmoded,

◀

**WINE SKIN**

A goat skin on display at Qatrin in Golan.

but because the new packs such power that the old cannot contain it.

## Plucking Grain on the Sabbath (2:23 – 28)

**They began to pick some heads of grain (2:23).** Fields were not fenced but marked out by stones, so that taking shortcuts through planted fields was not unusual. The disciples may have followed a path

---

## ▶ The Sabbath

The Sabbath was fundamental to Judaism as a sign of Israel's sanctification among all the nations. (1) It marked a joyful entry into sacred time (the time of the beginning before human work) and divine repose. Josephus claimed that "the word Sabbath in the Jew's language denotes cessation from all work."[A-10] (2) It allowed the people to honor God's holiness, who sanctified this day.[A-11] (3) It set Israel apart from the nations and served as a bulwark against assimilation to pagan culture. Keeping the Sabbath became a profession of faith. (4) Desecrating the Sabbath was akin to dishonoring the covenant (Isa. 56:4 – 6) and was worthy of death.[A-12] It was believed to unleash God's judgment on Israel (Neh. 13:18). This last concern may have motivated the Pharisees' consternation over perceived Sabbath violations.

Pietist groups in Israel multiplied the strict rules related to Sabbath observance. The earliest list of restrictions are found in *Jubilees* 2:17 – 33; 50:6 – 13 and CD 10:14 – 11:18. The Mishnah, the collection of the oral tradition compiled sometime before A.D. 220, contains three tractates specifically addressing Sabbath issues: *Šabbat* (prohibitions of work and what objects may or may not be carried), *ʿErubin* (rules about extending the limits for movement on the Sabbath) and *Beṣah* (work permitted and prohibited on festivals). A rabbinic commentary on Exodus goes so far as to prohibit activities that merely detract from the restfulness of the day.[A-13] The rabbis recognized that the manifold Sabbath rules were only tenuously connected to scriptural law: "The rules about the sabbath, festal offerings and sacrilege are as mountains hanging by a hair, for Scripture is scanty and the rules many."[A-14]

already struck by others and plucked grain as they went, rubbing it together before eating. Deuteronomy 23:25 permits gathering grain in another's field, but the Pharisees accuse the disciples of violating the Sabbath by harvesting, that is, extracting the edible content from something that had not previously been set aside for Sabbath consumption.[72] The disciples may also have violated the prohibition of moving beyond fixed boundaries on the Sabbath (see Ex. 16:29).

The Pharisees' accusation derives from their interpretation of the law. They would prefer that the disciples fast rather than eat, but one was also not supposed to fast on the Sabbath.[73]

**In the days of Abiathar the high priest (2:26).** Abiathar was Ahimilech's son, who had escaped the massacre by Doeg the Edomite. According to 1 Samuel 21:1–6, Ahimilech, not Abiathar, was the one who gave the bread of the Presence to David. Abiathar, however, was the high priest particularly associated with David, and this reference may be an example of eponymous dating for this period — during the Abiathar era (compare Luke 3:2).

**The consecrated bread, which is lawful only for priests to eat (2:26).** The loaves

of presentation (Lev. 24:7–9) are set out before the Lord as an offering but belong to Aaron and his sons, who are to eat them in a holy place. The illustration from David is pertinent because he was not just any hungry man but God's anointed. His personal authority and the urgency of the situation made his violation of the law excusable. Jesus' argument assumes that if the regulations regarding the bread of the Presence could be set aside for David when he lied that the king had charged him with a mission (1 Sam. 21:2), how much more can holy regulations be set aside for one whom Mark has identified as the Messiah, the Son of God? His mission to proclaim the kingdom of God is not a falsehood and carries with it far greater urgency.

**The Sabbath was made for man (2:27).** Scholars have argued that rabbis would judge an appeal to 1 Samuel 21 to be invalid for establishing a legal precept regarding Sabbath observance. Historical passages could only be used to illustrate or corroborate a legal argument. This criticism, however, may help us see more clearly Jesus' purposes. He is not interested in convincing the hair-splitting legal experts but converting the more common-sense oriented masses.

**WHEAT**

*(left)* A wheat field.

*(right)* A close-up of grains of wheat.

▼

He also does not want to set up more rules to decide what can or cannot be done on the Sabbath but wants to penetrate through the rules to unfold God's will for the Sabbath. God did not create the Sabbath for humans to obey but for human well-being. One can never interpret the law correctly unless one refers back to God's intention behind the law. God intended the Sabbath as a gracious gift to release human beings from the necessity of endless toil. Jesus emphasizes that David "had need" and "was hungry" and that human need has priority over regulations. The incident reveals that something new has broken in, and Jesus rules over the rules. Disciples need not concern themselves about appearing to be irreligious when they are carrying out the greater task of doing God's will. There will be plenty of other Sabbaths to keep holy.

## Healing on the Sabbath (3:1 – 6)

**Another time he went into the synagogue, and a man with a shriveled hand was there (3:1).** The man with the shriveled hand would have stood out in the synagogue when the congregation rose and lifted their hands in prayer. A shriveled hand is frequently understood to be the punishment of God.[74] Jeroboam's hand "dried up" when he tried to take action against the rebellious prophets (1 Kings 13:4 – 6), and it was healed only after he pleaded that the prophet pray for his restoration.

**They watched him closely to see if he would heal him on the Sabbath (3:2).** Jesus makes the man the center of attention by calling him forward and healing him. This healing violates the Pharisees' interpretation that disallows minor cures on the Sabbath.[75] Rabbi Shammai was so strict that he is reported even to have opposed praying for the sick or visiting the sick on the Sabbath, since it conflicted with the day's character as one marked by joy.[76] All the later rabbis agreed that danger to life overrode the Sabbath; they only disagreed over the scriptural basis for this conclusion.[77] Since this man with a withered hand is not in a life or death situation, the opponents assume that he can and should wait for a cure.

But how does Jesus violate the Sabbath? He prepares no ointments and lifts nothing; he simply speaks. The text assumes that if this man's healing were not in accord with God's will, he would not have been healed. Jesus uses the healing to make the point that the Sabbath can become an occasion to do good rather than simply a time not to do work. Why should this man have to wait a day for help when the power to heal him is available now? The point: God did not send the Messiah to observe the Sabbath but to save life.

**The Herodians (3:6).** The precise identity of the Herodians (see also 12:13) is hazy. Most assume that they were supporters of the Herodian rule. In Galilee, they would be partisans of Herod Antipas and consequently influential. Economically and religiously they were comparable to the Sadducees, who had been pro-Hasmonean. Their agenda was less motivated by religious fervor than a concern to maintain the social and political status quo, which religion nicely abetted.

Others have guessed that "Herodians" was a tag that the common people gave to the Essenes. Josephus tells the story of an Essene teacher who won the favor of Herod the Great as a young boy by greeting him as king of the Jews and predicting a happy reign.[78] They became the favored religious party during his rule, inhabiting the Essene quarter in the southwest corner of Jerusalem.[79]

## Summary of Jesus' Healing (3:7 – 12)

**Many people came to him from Judea, Jerusalem, Idumea, and the regions across the Jordan and around Tyre and Sidon (3:8).** The multitudes pressing on Jesus come from places that correspond to the land of biblical Israel. They swarm around the house he is in so that he is unable even to eat (3:20). This makes it necessary for him to prepare an escape route by boat (3:9).

**Whenever the evil spirits saw him, they fell down before him and cried out, "You are the Son of God" (3:11).** Only the demons know who Jesus really is, but

they can never be agents of revelation. In the first-century setting, most would have considered it ominous for demons to shout out a name in recognition (see comments on 1:24). They would not assume that demons were paying Jesus homage but that they were attempting to control him by pronouncing his divine name. Jesus' rebuke shows his power over them.

## Calling of Disciples on the Mountain (3:13 – 19)

**Jesus went up on a mountainside (3:13).** Mark does not identify the mountain where Jesus calls the twelve disciples. Mountains serve in the Bible as places of revelation, but the mountain here is simply an isolated place that allows Jesus to be alone. Crowds do not follow him here; he calls those whom he wants.

**He appointed twelve — designating them apostles (3:14).** "Twelve" has symbolic significance, evoking God's promises of redeeming Israel. God commanded Moses to take men from each tribe to be "with him" as representatives of the "heads of the clans of Israel."[80] The twelve disciples represent the heads of the divisions of Israel, which are being restored; and Jesus stands over them as leader. His choice of twelve testifies to his self-understanding that he has been sent to gather Israel.

**Simon (to whom he gave the name Peter) (3:16).** Simon, James, and John head the list as the three most prominent disciples and appear at significant junctures in the story. Simon was a popular name and nearly all the Simons mentioned in the New Testament are given some distinguishing name: for example, Simon the Cananaean (3:18; NIV, the Zealot), Simon the Leper (14:3), Simon of Cyrene (15:21), Simon the Pharisee (Luke 7:40), Simon Iscariot (John 6:71), Simon the sorcerer (Acts 8:9), Simon the tanner (Acts 9:43), and Jesus' brother Simon (Mark 6:3). In the biblical tradition, however, God or a divine agent gives new names to persons who will have a significant role in the story of God's people.[81] When someone in the Bible is given a different name, it represents a promise to that person (see Gen. 17:15; 32:28).

Jesus calls Simon *petros.* The word *petros* in Greek usually means a free standing "stone" that can be picked up. The word *petra* usually means rock, cliff, or bedrock (see Matt. 7:24). Both terms could reverse their meanings, and no clear-cut distinction can be made between the two.[82] A rock could serve as a foundation or security, but it could also become a rock of stumbling and an obstacle to agriculture (Mark 4:16).

**Boanerges, which means Sons of Thunder (3:17).** James and John, previously introduced as the sons of Zebedee, are now presented as "Sons of Thunder." The word *Boanerges* means nothing in Greek and it is unclear what Aramaic phrase it might transliterate. It may imply excitability or anger (see Luke 9:54), but this is uncertain. God's voice is referred to as thunderous (Ps. 29:3), and in Revelation 16:18, the final judgment is ushered in with peals of thunder.

**Simon the Zealot (3:18).** The translation follows Luke 6:15 (Acts 1:13), but the text reads literally Simon the Cananaean. We are not to think that he was a revolutionary. The term *qannaîm* appears in rabbinic sources to refer to those who were especially zealous for the law and its observance. This notion may be connected to his label (see Gal. 1:14).

**Judas Iscariot (3:19).** The name may mean "man of Kerioth." Textual variants found in John 6:71; 12:4; 13:2; and 14:22 add *apo Karyomtou* (from Kariot), which represent an early explanation for the term's meaning. Kerioth could be a town in Moab (Jer. 48:24; Amos 2:2) or a town in southern Judea (Josh. 15:25). If this reading is correct, Judas would have been in the minority as a Judean among Jesus' Galilean disciples. Other less likely suggestions contend that the name refers to his membership in a group of assassins ("dagger man," *sicarius*) or a clan ("man of Issachar"), his deceit ("the false one"), his betrayal ("the one handing over"), his origin ("man from the city"), or his ruddy complexion.

Mention of betrayal hints of the death that awaits Jesus. Judas does not worm his way into the inner circle but is chosen by Jesus from the beginning. Jesus' culture cherished loyalty and trust and abhorred treachery that shreds the fabric of a close-knit community. Betrayal was regarded as inexcusable and unforgivable.

## The Reaction of Family and Teachers of the Law (3:20 – 35)

Two groups try to quash Jesus' ministry for different reasons. His family seeks to protect him from danger and to protect the family honor, thinking that he is out of his mind. Teachers of the law from Jerusalem try to dishonor him with the people, claiming he works by Beelzebub.

**He is possessed by Beelzebub! (3:22).** The text reads literally, "He has Beelzebub," which parallels the charge that he has an unclean spirit (3:30). The origin of the term Beelzebub is vague, but it clearly is connected to "the prince of demons." The name may be a perversion of the name of a Philistine deity lampooned as "the lord of the flies." Beelzebul (which some MSS. read here) is identified as the prince of the demons in the *Testament of Solomon* 2:9 – 4:2. According to a rabbinic tradition, Jesus was condemned to death for practicing sorcery and misleading the people:

It has been taught: On the eve of Passover they hanged Yeshu. And an announcer went out, in front of him, for fourteen days [saying]: "He is going to be stoned because he practiced sorcery."[83]

This tradition independently confirms that Jesus was well known for doing miracles even though it attributes the source of his wonders to an evil power.

**How can Satan drive out Satan? (3:23).** Jesus' opponents concede that he is a successful exorcist, but they deliberately attempt to undermine him by labeling him as evil. Describing the enemy as subhuman or evil in some way makes it easier to justify doing away with him. They assume that someone who flouts his hallowed traditions can only be an undercover agent for Satan or for one who has made a compact with Satan.

Jesus exposes how absurd their accusation is. If they are correct, it must mean that civil war erupted in the ranks of Satan. Would Satan try to do himself in? Would he grant satanic power to someone to decimate his own minions? Satan extends his kingdom by sowing chaos and enslaving humans, not by setting them free. If it is unlikely that these exorcisms are worked by Satan's power, then how is it happening? Jesus answers only indirectly with an allegory about a stronger one who binds the previously reigning strong man and pillages his house. In Jesus' allegory, the strong one is Satan. His house is his domain, the present world he seeks to hold secure. His vessels are those hapless victims whom he has taken captive. The stronger one is Jesus, who has come from God (see 1:7; also Isa. 49:24 – 25), invaded Satan's stronghold, and bound him. Anyone with common sense would recognize that exorcisms bring healing, not harm. These opponents obdurately refuse to recognize that Jesus' ministry has to do with the collapse of Satan's kingdom, not its upsurge. Ironically, these experts from Jerusalem who seek to sabotage Jesus' ministry and blacken his reputation are the ones siding with the forces of Satan.

**Whoever blasphemes against the Holy Spirit will never be forgiven (3:28).** God is at work in Jesus. The sin referred to is willfully and spitefully denying the activity of God's Spirit in the ministry of Jesus and labeling it an unclean spirit. Jesus uses hyperbole to make his point and warn his listeners of its severity. In the Old Testament, defiant, high-handed sin is labeled unpardonable.[84] McNeile comments: "If the Lord spoke as a Jew to Jews and used the type of expression current in His day, and derived from the Old Testament, He meant, and would be understood to mean,

## REFLECTIONS

**OBEYING JESUS' CALL CREATES** family relationships within the community of God that transcend the boundaries of blood and marriage, the clan, and the nuclear family. Jesus does not mean that Christians do not need or should not have special people in their lives, but he does anticipate that his community will embrace and nurture all who belong to him, especially those who may have no other family.

no more than that blasphemy against the Holy Spirit, by whose power He worked, was a terrible sin — more terrible than blasphemy against man."[85]

**Who are my mother and my brothers? (3:33).** In Jesus' world, people did not think of themselves as individuals but as members of a primary group, usually the family. Jesus' behavior brought unwanted attention to the family and dishonor since the accusations against him also reflect directly on them.

## Parables Beside the Sea (4:1 – 34)

**Again Jesus began to teach by the lake (4:1).** Jesus' power exerts such a magnetic attraction that he speaks from a boat to crowds massed on the shore. A sloping amphitheater-like inlet lies halfway between Capernaum and Tabgha and has excellent natural acoustics, allowing someone to be heard easily on the shoreline. Jesus may have used this cove in teaching the crowds.

**He taught them many things by parables (4:2).** Parables are not simply illustrative yarns or earthly stories with heavenly meanings. The Hebrew *mashal* provides the backdrop for Jesus' parables. It "can mean a dark, perplexing saying that is meant to stimulate hard thinking."[86] The parables are "the opposite of prosaic, propositional teaching" and "attract attention by their pictorial or paradoxical language, and at the same time their indirect approach serves to tease and provoke the hearer."[87] They reveal the mystery while hiding it at the same time because a listener can only understand them by daring to become involved in their imaginative world. Even then, understanding the parables requires special help (4:33).

**Listen! A farmer went out to sow his seed (4:3).** In the Greco-Roman world, sower was a stock symbol for a teacher, sowing for teaching, seed for words, and soils for students.[88] These parallel ideas contrast with Jesus' parable. The Hellenistic writers compare farming to learning and refer to cultivation, toil, achievement, reward, and virtue. What stifles the seed from growing is a lack of intellect. The interpretation of Jesus' parable does not attribute the loss to some intellectual deficit. The failures are caused by cosmic forces — Satan snatching the seed; social forces — withering under persecution; and ethical breakdowns — temporal anxieties and the lure of riches. The reason for the failure of the seed is the lamentable spiritual state of the hearer's heart, not the lamentable state of the hearer's mind.[89]

A second difference is that sowing in Scripture is a metaphor for God's work. God promises to sow Israel to begin her renewal. In *4 Ezra* 8:6, the seed is understood as spiritual seed. God says, "For I sow my law in you, and it shall bring forth fruit in you, and you shall be glorified through it forever."[90] The reference to sowing, therefore, brings up three motifs. (1) It recalls God's promise of an end-time Israel planted by God. According to the vision in *1 Enoch* 62:8, "the congregation of the holy ones shall be planted [lit., sown], and all the elect ones shall stand before him." (2) Since sowing is a metaphor for God's work, this parable does not illustrate the effect that any teacher may have on pupils as in the Hellenistic parallels. It defines Jesus' ministry and implies that he comes as the end-time sower to renew Israel. How one responds to his teaching decides whether one will be included in God's kingdom. (3) The seeds sown are not just nuggets of wisdom. The seed is God's word, and God says, "It will not return to me empty, but will accomplish what I desire and achieve the purpose for which I sent it" (Isa. 55:11).

**Some fell along the path. . . . Some fell on rocky places. . . . Other seed fell among thorns (4:4 – 7).** The parable pictures a farmer working marginal ground using a broadcast method of sowing where seeds fall everywhere — on the path, on rocky ground, and among thorns. What field in Palestine did not have its rocks and thorns and thistles? All seed sown does not prosper (*4 Ezra* 8:41), but against formidable odds, the miracle of a harvest will occur.

Some have tried to explain away the seeming carelessness of a farmer who casts good seed on the pathway, on a rocky substratum, and among thorn bushes to make the parable more realistic and less allegorical. They argue that plowing did not precede sowing, and the sower would later plow the seed into the ground. It would not help to plow thorns under, however, since they would only sprout up again. A pathway established by villagers would only be trampled down again.

Sowing did not always precede plowing.[91] One expert maintains that sowing may precede plowing only if the soil is silty or loamy and will form an even tilth when plowed. "Under any other soil conditions sowing in unploughed stubble would be condemned by any competent authority as a wasteful and slovenly proceeding."[92] This comports with the exhortation in Jeremiah: "This is what the LORD says to the men of Judah and to Jerusalem: 'Break up your unplowed ground and do not sow among thorns' " (Jer. 4:3).

**It came up, grew and produced a crop, multiplying thirty, sixty, or even a hundred times (4:8).** The harvest numbers do not refer to the bulk yield of the whole field. That was calculated from the proportion of the amount of seed sown to grain threshed. The varied yield refers instead to the numbers of grains produced by individual plants. Pliny mentioned that wheat with branching ears yielded a hundred grains.[93] Modern agronomists assert that wheat normally produces "two or three tillers under typical crowded field conditions, but individual plants on fertile soil with ample space may produce as many as 30 to 100 hundred tillers. The average spike (head) of common wheat contains 25 to 30 grains in 14 to 17 spikelets. Large spikes may contain 50 to 75 grains."[94] Wheat grown in ancient times approached these numbers. Strabo wrote that a deputy governor of a region in Africa reported to the emperor the incredible result of 400 shoots obtained from a single grain of seed and sent to Nero also 360 stalks obtained from one grain. He then reports that "at all events the plains of Lentini and other districts in Sicily, and the whole of Andalusia, and particularly Egypt reproduce at the rate of a hundredfold."[95]

## REFLECTIONS

**JESUS' DISCIPLES ARE TO CONTINUE THE TASK OF** sowing, and this parable provides a note of encouragement for the sower and warning to the soil. The sower in this parable is not responsible for success but only for sowing. We should mark that the sower does not prejudge the soil's potential before casting the seed but sows with abandon. Sowing will not meet with universal success, but no farmer refrains from scattering the seed out of fear that some might be wasted. Success comes from God (1 Cor. 3:5 – 9), and contemporary sowers are called only to be faithful in the task and to allow the seed to do its work. The parable also identifies, and therefore warns about, conditions that make bad soil barren. It does not say what makes productive soil good except to caution listeners to be careful how they hear.

**The secret of the kingdom of God (4:11).** Because the parables are characterized as secret, everyone needs Jesus' interpretation to unlock the mystery. The word translated "secret" is "mystery." It does not refer to something baffling or unintelligible but to something that could not be known except by divine revelation. Behind this concept is the Old Testament idea of God's secret that cannot be discovered by human wisdom but can only be revealed by God. What was once hidden — how God is establishing his sovereignty over the world — is now being revealed.[96]

The idea that many remain in the dark is familiar in Jewish apocalyptic ("You do not reveal your mysteries to many," *2 Bar.* 48:2 – 3). We find a similar idea expressed in the Dead Sea Scrolls. The wicked are those who have not inquired nor sought God "to know the hidden matters in which they err."[97] The outsiders' unbelief is therefore not caused by the parables' obscurity but by their unwillingness to try to stretch their minds around Jesus' unconventional visions of God's kingdom. Insiders want to know more and come to him to ask for clarification.

**Satan comes and takes away the word that was sown in them (4:15).** Ancient Jewish texts also liken Satan to a bird or birds.[98] *Second Enoch* 29:5 pictures Satan's expulsion from heaven as resulting in his flight: "And I threw him out from the height with his angels, and he was flying in the air continuously above the bottomless."

**Do you bring in a lamp to put it under a bowl or a bed? (4:21).** Lamps were associated with gladness and marriage and were also important in the religious life of the Jewish household.[99] The Sabbath lamp was lit at dusk since fire could not be kindled on the Sabbath (Ex. 35:3), the Day of Atonement, or the Passover. The words of the prophets are likened to a light shining in a dark place (2 Peter 1:19). In *4 Ezra* 12:42, Ezra is compared to a lamp in a dark place (and a haven for a ship saved from a storm).

## REFLECTIONS

**THE PARABLE REMINDS US THAT** we live in the in-between-time, when humans tend to overlook God's reign or dismiss it as inconsequential or lacking certifiable proof. Before one can see how God's purposes are being accomplished in the world through the cross of Christ, one needs spiritual discernment, given only by God.

ANCIENT OIL LAMPS

▼

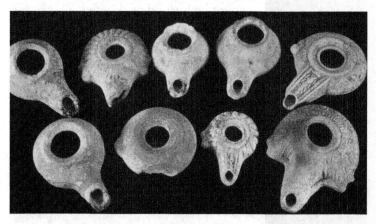

**With the measure you use, it will be measured to you — and even more (4:24).** This parable affirms that those who do not hear rightly will become have-nots who lose everything. Those who hear well will receive more explanation and understanding. A rabbinic tradition professes:

Observe how the character of the Holy One, blessed be He, differs from that of flesh and blood. A mortal can put something into an empty vessel, but not into a full one. But the Holy One, blessed be He, is not so; He puts more into a full vessel, but not an empty one; for it says, "If hearkening you will hearken" (Ex. 15:26), implying, if you hearken you will go on hearkening, and if not you will not hearken.[100]

**A man scatters seed on the ground (4:26).** Jesus again compares the things of God to the everyday world of a farmer in the only parable peculiar to Mark. It reflects a Palestinian perspective. The farmer first sleeps and then rises because the day begins in the evening, not in the morning.

**All by itself the soil produces grain (4:28).** The seed holds within itself the secret of its growth that follows an appointed order of development that cannot be hurried or skipped. This parable expresses the belief that the growth of plants is the wondrous work of God. His purposes will be fulfilled in his way and his time.

**It is like a mustard seed, which is the smallest seed you plant in the ground (4:31).** The mustard seed was proverbi-

ally small (see Matt. 17:20, "if you have faith as small as a mustard seed"). The Mishnah uses the phrase "even as little as a grain of mustard" to describe the smallest possible quantity.[101] It requires 725 – 760 seeds from the black mustard to make a gram.[102] The parable contrasts the mustard bush's microscopic beginning with its lush outcome. The kingdom of God is something present and yet something that will be transformed and is therefore yet to come. The present activity of God, "not the plausibility of the evidence, guarantees that great ending."[103]

**Yet when planted, it grows and becomes the largest of all garden plants, with such big branches that the birds of the air can perch in its shade (4:32).** The mustard bush was cultivated in the field (Matt. 13:31) and grown for its leaves as well as its grains. Wild mustard (charlock) was unwelcome since it was almost impossible to get rid of it. Pliny claims that "mustard . . . with its pungent taste and fiery effect is extremely beneficial for the health. It grows entirely wild, though it is improved by being transplanted: but on the other hand when it has once been sown it is scarcely possible to get the

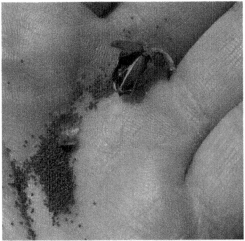

place free of it, as the seed when it falls germinates at once."[104]

The NIV translation of the verb *kataskēnoō* as "perch" is based on the assumption that the mustard bush was hardly a suitable place for the birds of the air to nest. It is a fast-growing annual plant that grows to a height of eight to ten feet. Spring is the time when birds build their nests, but the mustard has not yet grown large enough for the birds to build nests in its branches.[105] It is assumed that the birds are attracted to the bush by the seeds. But the verb means to dwell, lodge, or nest. The noun form *kataskēnōsis* is used for bird nests in Matthew 8:20 and Luke 9:58. The image recalls Old Testament texts. Daniel 4:12, 21 refers to a tree in which "the birds of the air" have nesting places. In Ezekiel 17:23 and 31:6, God promises to plant a noble cedar on the mountain height of Israel that towers over all the trees of the field, and in its boughs "birds of every kind will nest."[106]

The "birds of the air" was a transparent symbol for the nations of Gentiles.[107] The image of lodging or shelter appears in *Joseph and Asenath* 15:6 for the incorporation of the Gentiles in the people of God. After Asenath is converted, an angel appears to her and tells her that she will be given the name "City of Refuge, because in you many nations will take refuge with the Lord God, the Most High, and under your wings many peoples trusting in the Lord God will be sheltered [*kataskēnousi*]."

This background may point to more subtle meanings hidden in the parable of the mustard bush. The tree mentioned in the Old Testament is planted on a high and lofty mountain (Ezek. 17:22), and its top reaches to heaven so that it is visible to the ends of the earth (Dan. 4:11, 20). When one is talking about the kingdom of God and birds of heaven lodging under the protection of trees with great branches, the Jewish listener was conditioned by Scripture and tradition to think in terms of the salvation of pagans through Israel's triumph.[108] Does this parable cleverly undermine notions of grandeur with its jarring image of a mustard bush?

## The Stilling of the Storm (4:35 – 41)

**Let us go over to the other side (4:35).** The inclusion of "other boats" means that the group of insiders surrounding Jesus was not limited only to the twelve. The Sea of Galilee was also known as the Sea of Tiberias (John 21:1) and the Lake of Gennesaret.[109] It is thirteen miles long and seven miles wide. Going across to the other side of the lake is mentioned in Mark 4:35; 5:1, 21; 6:45; 8:13. Josephus describes the Jordan River as "cutting across the Lake" so that the river's entry and exit points "formed an imaginary line which determined whether a location was 'on the side' or 'on the other side' of the lake."[110]

**They took him along, just as he was, in the boat (4:36).** An ancient boat was discovered buried in the silt of this lake during

a prolonged dry season. It has allowed us the opportunity to picture exactly the kind of boat Jesus and his disciples would have sailed. Carbon 14 testing dates the boat from this time period, 120 B.C. to A.D. 40. An oil lamp inside the boat was dated to the mid-first century B.C., and coins from A.D. 29 – 30 were also found. The boat measured 25.5 feet long, 7.5 feet wide, and 4.5 feet in depth. It had a deck in the bow and the stern and could be powered by sails or by four oars. It normally would have a crew of five with a capacity for ten passengers or in excess of a ton of cargo.[111]

**A furious squall came up (4:37).** Two extensive valleys on the western side of the lake funnel wind onto the lake. Westerly gusts can arise in the afternoon, turning the placid lake into a high sea with waves soaring up over seven feet.[112] The lake also is 682 feet below sea level, which makes it susceptible to downdrafts when "cool air from the Golan Heights meets the warm air coming off the lake, and these contribute to sudden and unpredictable storms."[113] Sudden storms are therefore familiar sailing hazards.

**Jesus was in the stern, sleeping on a cushion (4:38).** Jesus has probably fallen asleep under the stern deck, which

affords the most protection from the elements and keeps him out of the way of those sailing the vessel. The "cushion" is probably a sandbag used for ballast. Two types were used: a sack of a hundred to a hundred and twenty pounds; and a pillow of around fifty pounds.

The storm at sea should be read against an Old Testament backdrop. Jonah was in a deep sleep in the midst of a storm that terrified the sailors. In Psalm 107:23 – 32, imperiled sailors cry out to the Lord in their trouble, and he "stilled the storm to a whisper; the waves of the sea were hushed."[114] The incident reveals that Jesus has mastery over the sea, the place of chaos and evil, as does God. Jesus awakes to muzzle the sea in the same way he rebuked demons (1:25; 3:12; 9:25).[115] His sleep during the storm contrasts with the disciples' terror. God "grants sleep to those he loves" (Ps. 127:2), and Jesus' sleep reflects his serene trust in God, who watches over him.[116]

## The Gerasene Demoniac (5:1 – 20)

**They went across the lake to the region of the Gerasenes (5:1).** Gerasa, modern Jerash, was thirty miles from the lake. That distance from the sea probably prompted the textual variants locating the incident at Gadara or Gergesa. Some have suggested that the original reference was to a town that is now called Kersa or Koursi, which was later mistaken for the better-known Gerasa, a member of the Decapolis. Most likely, however, this is territory controlled by Gerasa, which extends to the Sea of Galilee.

**This man lived in the tombs, and no one could bind him any more, not even with a chain (5:3).** Mark emphasizes both the fierce strength of the man, who could

**GALILEE**

Gergesa and Gadara were located east of the Sea of Galilee. Jerash was about 40 miles southeast of the sea (off this map).

▼

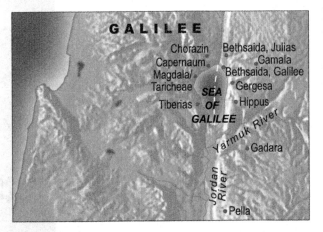

not be subdued even with chains, and the drastic nature of his possession, which drove him to lacerate himself. In the New Testament, demoniacs are never aggressive, unless one interferes with them. Rather, they are victims who need an external power to liberate them from their thralldom.

This demonized soul, screaming in his tortured isolation, lives in the unclean place of the dead and has become himself a dwelling place for unclean spirits. Tombs were frequently located in caves and were known as haunts for demons.[117] The man fits the four characteristics of madness found in rabbinic literature: running about at night, staying overnight in burial places, tearing apart one's clothes, and destroying what one has been given.[118]

**What do you want with me, Jesus, Son of the Most High God? Swear to God that you won't torture me! (5:7).** Unlike humans, who never quite fathom the reality of the divine breaking into human history (4:41), the unclean spirits always recognize Jesus' divine origin and his threat to them (1:24; 3:11; see James 2:19). Ancient listeners to this account would have recognized the irony that these demons attempt to resist exorcism with gimmicks from an exorcist's bag of tricks. They attempt to control Jesus by pronouncing aloud his holy name. Knowing the names of demons was believed to give one control over them.[119] Ironically, they try to invoke the name of God to protect themselves.

**"What is your name?" ... "My name is Legion" (5:9).** Jesus counters these diversionary tactics by asking for the demon's name. The unclean spirits evade the question by giving a number instead of a name. "Legion" was the term for a Roman regiment commanded by a senator of praetorian rank and generally consisting of 5,400 foot soldiers and 120 horsemen. The man was possessed by an army of demons.

**The demons begged Jesus, "Send us among the pigs; allow us to go into them" (5:12).** Ancients understood that demons always want to inhabit something rather than wander about aimlessly.[120] Some were thought to be land demons, who would be destroyed in water. In the *Testament of Solomon* 5:11 (see 11:6), a demon about to be exorcised pleads: "Do not condemn me to water."

The enormously large herd of 2,000 pigs grubbing on the hillside must have belonged to a swine cooperative and marks this as a pagan area. Isaiah lumps

▶ **A Spell for Driving out Daimons from the Greek Magical Papyri**

Place an olive branch before him and stand behind him and say:

Hail, God of Abraham; hail, God of Isaac, God of Jacob; Jesus Chrestos [excellent one], the Holy Spirit, the Son of the Father, who is above the Seven, who is within the Seven. Bring Iao Sabaoth; may your power issue forth from him, [name to be inserted], until you drive away this unclean daimon Satan who is in him. I conjure you, daimon, whoever you are, by this God, SABARBARBATHIOMTH SABARBARBATHIOUTH SABARBARBATHIOMNEMTH SABARBARBAPHAI. Come out, daimon, whoever you are, and stay away from him, [name to be inserted] now, now; immediately, immediately. Come out, daimon, since I bind you with unbreakable adamantine fetters, and I deliver you into the black chaos in perdition.[A-15]

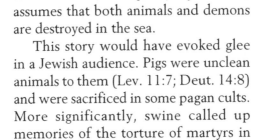

the days of Antiochus Epiphanes. He had polluted the temple by sacrificing swine on the altar and attempted to eradicate Jewish distinctives with a savage campaign of persecution (1 Macc. 1:41 – 61). During this time, abstaining from eating pork became compelling proof of loyalty to God.[121] Swine were thus associated with pagan attempts to abolish Judaism.

Those reading this story after the destruction of Jerusalem may have made another connection. The Tenth Roman Legion (Fretensis) took part in the sieges of Jerusalem and Masada and was stationed in Jerusalem after its fall. Its standards bore the image of a wild boar. According to Josephus, it had a complement of a thousand horses and two thousand foot soldiers.[122] Many Jews would have liked nothing better than to see this Roman legion — guilty of defiling the land, destroying the holy city, and killing and enslaving thousands — driven into the sea.

pork eaters, tomb dwellers, and demon worshipers together (Isa. 65:3 – 4). Demons try to destroy whatever they inhabit and never leave their victims quietly (Mark 1:26; 9:26). When Jesus grants the demons' request to enter into the pigs, these very un-herdlike animals stampede down the bank and into the waters, where Jesus has just demonstrated his dominion (4:39, 41). The text assumes that both animals and demons are destroyed in the sea.

This story would have evoked glee in a Jewish audience. Pigs were unclean animals to them (Lev. 11:7; Deut. 14:8) and were sacrificed in some pagan cults. More significantly, swine called up memories of the torture of martyrs in

**So the man went away and began to tell in the Decapolis how much Jesus had done for him (5:20).** The Decapolis was a league of free Greek cities under the protection of the Roman governor of Syria: Damascus, Raphana, Dion, Canantha, Scythopolis, Gadar, Hippos, Pella, Gerasa, and Philadelphia. The great calm that came over the sea matches the great calm that now governs the man, sitting quietly and fully clothed at Jesus' feet. The man's deliverance will spread the word into the heavily pagan Decapolis.

## Jairus' Daughter and the Woman with the Flow of Blood (5:21 – 43)

**Then one of the synagogue rulers, named Jairus, came there (5:22).** Jairus is a male leader of the synagogue and Mark iden-

tifies him by name. The woman with the flow of blood is nameless, and her complaint renders her ritually unclean, making her unfit to enter into a synagogue or the temple. The two individuals come from opposite ends of the social and purity spectrum.

**And a woman was there who had been subject to bleeding for twelve years (5:25).** The text does not specify the nature of the woman's loss of blood, but we can presume that it was related to uterine bleeding. Menstruation was a normal part of life that, nevertheless, made a woman unclean and confined her to home (see Ezek. 36:17). Leviticus 15:19 – 24 deals with normal female discharges. Her family was to refrain from lying in her bed, sitting on her seat, or touching her. Those contaminated by her had to purify themselves by bathing and laundering their clothes and remained unclean until the evening.

Outside of Judaism, Pliny reported that the touch of a menstruating woman was considered harmful.[123] An extreme view is found in the sectarian Ramban, who said that such women were not to approach people or speak with them because their breath is harmful and their gaze detrimental. Learned men were forbidden to greet a menstruant, or to walk after her and tread in her footsteps.[124]

This woman's condition was abnormal, making her unclean all the time. It would not have been kept secret in a small village society. She was subject to regulations listed in Leviticus 15:25 – 31, which sought to prevent impurity from infringing on the realm of God's holiness. As a bearer of such impurity, she was not permitted to participate in the religious feasts or enter the temple precincts,[125] and she was excluded from normal social

intercourse for twelve years. Such an affliction must have caused her physical, psychological, social, and economic suffering. Jesus' healing demonstrates that God's holiness cleanses human impurity and restores individuals to wholeness.

**She had suffered a great deal under the care of many doctors and had spent all she had (5:26).** Only the wealthy could afford the care of physicians, and now this woman has become impoverished (cf. Tobit 2:10). Doctors were not always revered.[126] We find complaints about their fees,[127] statements that even the best of doctors are destined for hell,[128] and advice not to stay in a town where the leading citizen is a physician.[129] A list of procedures for curing a woman who suffers from a flow of blood appears in the Babylonian Talmud. Possibly this poor woman endured some of them:

Let them procure three kapiza of Persian onions, boil them in wine, make her drink it, and say to her, "Cease your discharge." But if not, she should be made to sit at cross-roads, hold a cup of wine in her hand, and a man comes up from behind, frightens her and exclaims, "Cease your discharge!" But if not, a handful of cummin, a handful of saffron, and a handful of fenugreek are brought and boiled in wine, she is made to drink it, and they say to her, "Cease your discharge." But if not, let sixty pieces of sealing clay of a [wine] vessel be brought, and let them smear her and say to her, "Cease your discharge."

It offers five more remedies; the last suggests fetching a barley grain from the dung of a white mule. When she eats it and holds it in one day, her discharge will cease for one day, if for two days, her discharge will cease for two days, if for three days, it will cease forever.[130]

When she heard about Jesus, she came up behind him in the crowd and touched his cloak (5:27). In popular belief, the clothes of holy men, and especially the fringes, were thought to possess miraculous power. Touching Jesus' garment is mentioned four times here (5:27, 28, 30, 31). Already in 3:10, many who suffered diseases pushed forward to touch him. In 6:56, they beg him to let them touch the hem of his cloak, and all who touch him are healed. The belief that the power of a person is transferred to what he wears or touches is also found in Acts 5:15 and 19:12. To touch a man in public would have been highly irregular, and this woman tries to do it on the sly.

Daughter, your faith has healed you (5:34). God controls the power residing in Jesus, for the emphasis in this story is placed on the woman's faith, not on Jesus' power. Faith transfers divine power to those who are utterly powerless. When a woman was healed from this type of affliction, she was supposed to bring a sacrifice (Lev. 15:29 – 30), but Jesus makes no mention of this as he did for the leper (Mark 1:44). The miracle nicely dovetails with the next miracle. The woman's faith in Jesus reverses the loss of blood that betokened the ebbing away of life. Resurrection awaits all those who trust in Jesus, but even now they can see the forces of death being held at bay through their faith.

Your daughter is dead (5:35). Child mortality rate was high in this era. Sixty percent of children who survived childbirth died by their mid-teens.

*right* ▶

GALILEE

Jesus saw a commotion, with people crying and wailing loudly (5:38). Burial was swift, usually on the same day of death, and relatives, neighbors, and mourners were employed for the occasion and gathered quickly to make loud, theatrical demonstrations of sorrow (see Jer. 9:17 – 19).

He took her by the hand and said to her, "Talitha koum!" (5:41). *Talitha koum* is an ordinary Aramaic phrase made memorable by the extraordinary miracle.[131] By providing the translation, "Little girl, rise," Mark makes it clear that it was not some arcane, magical formula. Eating food proves that the child is really alive and not some disembodied spirit (cf. Luke 24:39 – 43).

## Jesus Dismissed by His Own (6:1 – 6)

Jesus left there and went to his hometown (6:1). Nazareth was located in the hills of Galilee and had a population of approximately 150 – 200 people. It was within an hour's walking distance of the large city of Sepphoris. It receives notice only in the New Testament and is not mentioned in the Old Testament, Apocrypha, or rabbinic literature.

Jesus alludes to his kinsmen and his house in 6:4. The clan members were descendants of King David, who possibly settled here after returning from the Babylonian exile. They may have given the

GALILEE
Gischala
Chorazin  Bethsaida, Julias
Capernaum
Gamala
Magdala/
Bethsaida, Galilee
Cana of Galilee  Taricheae  SEA
Tiberias  OF
Sepphoris  GALILEE
Nazareth
Mt. Tabor ▲
Nain
Jordan River

place an intentionally messianic name, Little-Netzer (offshoot [of David]), under the influence of Isaiah 11:1 – 2.[132]

**Isn't this the carpenter? (6:3).** When Jesus teaches in the synagogue, the astonishment of the "many," a Semitism for "all" (10:45), quickly turns into suspicion. Where did he come by all this? A lowborn village artisan had no business becoming a public figure. Jesus has stepped outside the bounds of his honor rating. "Isn't this the carpenter?" is therefore a sneer. In a later tale, Asenath angrily scorns Joseph as a potential husband by saying, "Is he not the shepherd's son from the land of Canaan?"[133]

The noun translated "carpenter" (*tektōn*) refers to someone who works with hard materials: wood, metal, stone. If Jesus were a carpenter, as tradition assumes, he would have been engaged in making farm tools such as plows, yokes, carts, wheels, winnowing forks, and threshing boards, as well as house parts, doors, frames, locks, window lattices, beds, tables, lampstands, boxes, cabinets, and chests. He also may have built and repaired boats. The excavated Galilean boat had been repaired often. Meier asserts: "The airy weakling often presented to us in pious paintings and Hollywood movies would hardly have survived the rigors of being Nazareth's *tektōn* from his youth to his early thirties."[134]

In the Greco-Roman world, most would have regarded a person in such a craft as uneducated and uncouth. Secundus (an Athenian orator) was mocked as a "wooden nail" because he was the son of a carpenter. Celsus derides Jesus for having been simply a carpenter, connecting his work to his crucifixion; Origen weakly counters that the Gospels never describe Jesus as working with his hands.[135] In Sirach 38:24 – 32, the skill-ful artisan who works with his hands is commended, but it is assumed that his business keeps him from ever becoming wise like the scribe. The scribe has greater leisure and can devote himself to the study of the law to gain greater wisdom (Sir. 39:1 – 11).

**Isn't this Mary's son? (6:3).** A man was normally identified as the son of his father. To be identified only as the son of the mother could be an insult (see Judg. 11:1 – 2), but there is no grounds to claim that it intimates some confusion about Jesus' father's identity. Possibly, the brothers and sisters listed were the children of Joseph's hypothetical first wife. Note that Mark uses the word "brother" in Mark 6:17 to identify the half brothers Herod Antipas and Herod Philip. Outside of Nazareth, where the family was unknown, Jesus would have been identified simply as the son of Joseph.[136] It seems more likely, however, that Jesus' father is no longer living. The townsfolk simply identify him as a "local boy" whose mother (and brothers and sisters) is well known.

**The brother of James, Joseph, Judas and Simon (6:3).** James (Jacob) and Joseph are the names of two of the patriarchs, and Judah and Simon are names of two of the famous Maccabee brothers. These names suggest a family that hoped for the redemption of Israel.

The argument that these are Jesus' cousins has been concocted to support the idea of Mary's perpetual virginity and has no basis in the Greek. Paul refers to James, whom he met, as "the Lord's brother" (Gal. 1:19), and to "the Lord's brothers" (1 Cor. 9:5); he does not use the Greek word for "cousins" (*anepsioi*), which he knows and uses elsewhere (Col. 4:10).[137]

**Aren't his sisters here with us? (6:3).** His sisters are unnamed and unnumbered, reflecting the ancient bias that females' identities are embedded in males and do not merit special attention.

## The Sending Out of the Disciples (6:7 – 13, 30)

**He sent them out two by two (6:7).** Sending the disciples two by two satisfies the requirement of two or three witnesses and provides them a measure of protection. Jesus' authority over unclean spirits is invested in the disciples (see 3:15).[138] In Numbers 27:20, some of Moses' dignity is invested in Joshua so that the Israelite community might obey him.

**Take nothing (6:8).** Jesus directs his disciples to take nothing normally required for trips: no bread, no satchel for provisions, no money (copper) in the belt, and no change of clothing. The disciples go unencumbered, entirely dependent on the hospitality of hosts, a virtue particularly cherished by Jews. They may take a staff, which may refer to the traveler's stick that Parrot describes as "a supple and flexible cane. When slipped behind the back under the arms, it works as a

**TYPICAL VILLAGE**

The village of Yata, near Hebron, that preserves the appearance of a typical ancient village in Judea.

▼

brace and makes one's gait more rapid and supple."[139] But the staff also has a rich imagery in the history of God's dealings with Israel, beginning with Moses' staff (Ex. 4:2 – 5, 20). The reference here may be connected to the staff of the twelve tribes (Num. 17), a symbol of a tribal leader's authority. It therefore may have some symbolic connection to the covenant renewal of Israel.[140]

**Shake the dust off your feet when you leave (6:11).** Jews shook the dust from their feet when they returned to Israel from Gentile territory.[141] The gesture may serve as a prophetic warning that the defiant will be cut off from Israel for failing to respond to the reign of God or as a sign that they were washing their hands of them (Acts 18:6), as if to say, "We do not even want your dust."

**Anointed many sick people with oil and healed them (6:13).** The *Testament of Solomon* is a collection of legends and beliefs that offers magical wisdom on how to exorcise demons. In 18:34, a demon that purportedly brings on long-term illnesses says, "If anyone puts salt into (olive) oil and massages his sickly (body with it) saying, 'Cherubim, seraphim, help (me),' I retreat immediately." The oil used by the disciples is probably olive oil, but they do not resort to magical healing arts. Jesus does not instruct them in any hocus-pocus. The oil may have been warmed and rubbed into the skin, and the human touch, not to mention prayer accompanying it, may have been part of the healing. Philo claims that olive oil was an excellent ointment that "produces smoothness, and counteracts physical exhaustion, and brings about good condition. If a muscle be relaxed it braces it and renders it firm, nor is there anything surpassing it for infusing tone and vigour."[142]

## The Death of John the Baptizer (6:14 – 29)

**King Herod heard about this, for Jesus' name had become well known (6:14).** The growing reputation of Jesus from his miracles causes jitters in Herod's court. A flashback relating the slaying of John the Baptizer explains the dread that Jesus may be the sequel: John the Baptist II.

**He had him bound and put in prison (6:17).** John's bold censure of the powerful Antipas earned him imprisonment. Josephus identifies the prison as Machaerus.[143] This fortress-palace (like Masada and Herodium) was situated atop a mountain in southeastern Perea, five miles east of the Dead Sea and thirteen miles southeast of Herodium. Josephus described the citadel as luxurious.[144]

Archaeologists have uncovered two large *triclinia* (dining rooms) that would have been suitable for a banquet and a small one where the women would have eaten during the banquet.

**He did this because of Herodias, his brother Philip's wife, whom he had married (6:17).** Herodias, the daughter of Aristobulus (son of Herod the Great) and Bernice (daughter of Herod the Great's sister, Salome), was married to Herod Philip, another son of Herod the Great. She was therefore the half niece of both Herods and the sister-in-law of Antipas. This Philip is not the

◀

COINS OF
HEROD PHILIP

## ▶ Herod Antipas

Herod the Great had ten wives, and every son had the name Herod as the family designation. Herod Antipas, whom Mark identifies only as Herod, was the son of Herod the Great and Malthace, a Samaritan. He was raised in Rome and served as "tetrarch" (ruler of a fourth part) of Galilee and Perea from 4 B.C. to A.D. 39.[A-16] Mark's mention of him as king may reflect popular usage or may be intentionally ironic. Augustus had specifically denied him that royal title when his father Herod died and his kingdom was carved up among his heirs.[A-17]

Herod Antipas's wife, Herodias, was exceedingly jealous when Herod Agrippa later received the title king from the emperor Gaius (Caligula). She egged on Antipas to request that the emperor also give him the title king. His ill-advised petition led to his dismissal and exile when opponents accused him of treachery against Rome in amassing a stockpile of weapons.[A-18]

Mark may be scornfully mocking Herod's royal pretensions by giving him the title he so coveted and that led to his ruin. Chapman aptly describes the Galilean dislike of Antipas:

The Jews hated his father. Antipas had close ties with Rome, and the Jews hated Rome. His mother was a Samaritan, and the Jews hated Samaritans. He built or rebuilt towns or cities naming them after *Roman* royalty. To populate Tiberias, he forcibly relocated his subjects (today's Palestinian controversy should cast light on how popular that move must have been). In Tiberias, he built a royal palace and adorned it with a frieze of animal figures, in violation of the Second Commandment.[A-19]

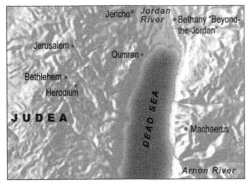

better known son of Herod and Cleopatra, who was the tetrarch. He is the son of Mariamne II and lived privately in Rome. When Herod Antipas was staying with them on a visit to Rome, he fell in love with Herodias and brazenly proposed marriage. She agreed upon the condition that he divorce his current wife, the daughter of Aretas IV, king of Nabatea. The outraged Aretas began a border war that led to serious military losses for Herod Antipas.[145] The divorce also touched off religious protests at home because marrying the wife of his half brother was forbidden and regarded as incest (Lev. 18:16; 20:21). Antipas would have deemed John's attack on his remarriage as a political threat.

Josephus and Mark recount John's death from different perspectives. Josephus claims that John was imprisoned and executed because Herod Antipas

feared the political unrest he aroused.[146] Mark reports that Herod executed John because of a public oath that leads him to bow to the will of Herodias.[147] Josephus has a marked interest in the suppression of potential uprisings, a critical Roman concern. Mark is primarily interested in the moral issues and the conniving of Herodias, which has biblical overtones. The Herodian family was infamous for its intrigues and grudges, and it is no surprise that Herodias conspired to destroy one who called for her removal from the halls of power. Josephus and Mark do not contradict each other; "political ends and the anger of an insulted woman cannot be regarded as mutually exclusive."[148]

**On his birthday Herod gave a banquet for his high officials and military commanders and the leading men of Galilee (6:21).** The account reeks of gross impiety. Birthdays were pagan celebrations.[149] Drunken revelry, a princess dancing at a stag party (she must leave to consult her mother), and execution without a trial all smack of rank paganism.[150] The grisly detail of John's head brought to them on a platter caps off a banquet already polluted by excess.

**Whatever you ask I will give you, up to half my kingdom (6:23).** As a puppet of Rome, Herod did not have the right to give half of his kingdom away. To preserve his honor by keeping his oath, Herod brings greater dishonor to his name.

## Feeding the Five Thousand (6:32 – 44)

**But many who saw them leaving recognized them and ran on foot from all the towns and got there ahead of them (6:33).** The crowd races around the lake

in its relentless pursuit of Jesus and beats the boat to its destination, further proof of Jesus' immense popularity. A tradition that the pilgrim Egeria (ca. 383 – 95) supports claims that the feeding took place at the Seven Springs, present-day Tabgha. Grass grows abundantly in this area. The crowd could hardly outrun the boat to the other side of the lake, a distance of fifteen to twenty miles. In springtime, the Jordan is high, and the crowds could not have easily crossed it.

**You give them something to eat (6:37).** The disciples want the crowds to go off to buy their own food and ask Jesus to send them away. Earlier they lived off the hospitality of others (6:8); now Jesus insists that they are to return the favor.

**Eight months of a man's wages (6:37).** Two hundred denarii is what this translates, which, according to Matthew 20:2, was a day's pay for a day laborer and would buy approximately 2400 loaves of bread, one-half inch thick and seven to eight inches in diameter.[151]

**They were like sheep without a shepherd (6:34).** The image of sheep without a shepherd echoes Moses' request for his successor when he is informed that he cannot lead them into the promised land (Num. 27:15 – 17). The shepherdless throng is soon organized by Jesus (see Ps. 23; Ezek. 34:23).

**So they sat down in groups of hundreds and fifties (6:40).** The assembly into orderly rows suggests the grouping of an army and recalls Israel's encampment.[152] Five thousand was also the typical number in a Roman legion and the number of Galilean troops Josephus said that he assembled for battle against the Romans in A.D. 67.[153] Rebel movements were known for gathering in the desert during this era, but Jesus is feeding a spiritual army, not a military company.

The feeding of bread and fish recalls several Old Testament themes. During Israel's sojourn in the desert God miraculously provided manna and quail. The disciple's astonished question when asked to feed the crowd parallels Moses' dismay at being asked to feed the people (Num. 11:22). The few small fish may connect to the complaints of Israel in the desert (11:4 – 6), and the collection of an abundance of leftovers shows that Jesus provides what Moses could not, bread that did not decay overnight. Unlike the disgruntled gathering around Moses, everyone is satisfied.

The feeding also challenges Roman propaganda. The Julia coins depict Livia, the wife of Augustus, as the goddess Demeter providing abundance. This miracle shows Jesus to be the true giver of bread.

## Walking on Water and Summary of Healings (6:45 – 56)

**Jesus made his disciples get into the boat and go on ahead of him to Bethsaida (6:45).** Bethsaida means "house of the fisher." It was located just east of the Jordan, so it qualified as being on "the other side" of the lake (see comments on 4:35). This is the first mention of Bethsaida (see 8:22), though the Gospel of John tells us that Jesus' disciples Philip, Andrew, and Peter hailed from there (John 1:44; 12:21). Jesus pronounces woes on the city and on Korazin (Matt. 11:20 – 22; Luke 10:13 – 14), condemning their failure to repent after the mighty works he had done there (see Mark 8:22 – 26).

Josephus credits Philip, the son of Herod the Great who was appointed Tetrarch of Batanea, Trachonitus, Auranitus, Gaulonitus (from 4 B.C. to

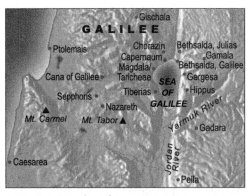

▶

**GALILEE**

Bethsaida was
located on the
north shore of the
Sea of Galilee. Gen-
nesaret was a plain
on the northwest
side of the Sea
between Tiberias
and Capernaum.

A.D. 33/34) by the emperor Augustus, for raising the village of Bethsaida to the status of a city and renaming it Julias to honor the emperor's daughter.[154] From the coin evidence, the dedication of the city does not appear to have occurred until A.D. 30. Presumably, the refounding of the city with extensive building projects and an influx of new settlers took place during Jesus' ministry.

Three sites have been connected with Bethsaida: et-Tell, now almost two miles from the lake, and el-Araj and el-Mess'adiyye on the lake's current shoreline. Geological evidence, however, indicates that in the past the sea or its estuaries extended closer to the base of the hill at et-Tell and that the shoreline, after two thousand years, has been altered by the passing of continental plates, earthquakes, floods, and silting.[155]

**After leaving them, he went up on a mountainside to pray (6:46).** Jesus disperses the crowds after they have eaten. Mark gives no explanation as to why he forces them into the boat (contrast John 6:15). If the tradition that places the feeding at Tabgha is correct, Jesus could go up the Eremos ridge and see the disciples struggling on the lake.

**About the fourth watch of the night he went out to them, walking on the lake (6:48).** Mark depicts Jesus as walking on the sea (not on the shore!). This account is not simply about rescuing the disciples in distress but describes the unveiling of Jesus as a heavenly figure. The scene is intended to hark back to Old Testament images of God as one who tramples the waves.[156] Jesus is more than a successor to Moses who fills up bread baskets in the desert; he is God with us.

**He was about to pass by them (6:48).** "He wanted to pass by them" accords with an Old Testament theophany scene where God parades by someone.[157] In Genesis 32:31 – 33 (LXX), the face of God "passed by" Jacob wrestling with the angel. By passing by, Jesus intends to reveal to them his transcendent majesty.

**When they saw him walking on the lake, they thought he was a ghost (6:49).** The sight of Jesus throws the disciples into a panic. According to Wisdom 17:3, 15, fearsome apparitions smite the wicked.

**"It is I" (6:50).** Jesus responds to their fear with the divine formula of self-revelation, "I am."[158] This self-revelation answers the disciples' question in 4:41, "Who is this? Even the wind and the waves obey him!" A rabbinic tradition has it that when waves that would sink a ship are struck with clubs on which is engraven " *'I am that I am,'* Yah, the Lord of Hosts, Amen, Amen, Selah," they subside.[159]

**When they had crossed over, they landed at Gennesaret and anchored there (6:53).** Jesus dispatched the disciples to Bethsaida (6:45), but they land in Gennesaret. Bethsaida was a town on the northeast side of the Sea of Galilee; Gennesaret probably refers to a district between Tiberias and Capernaum three and a half miles long and a mile wide on the northwest side of the sea. The district was a densely populated, fertile plain and included the city of Taricheae or Magdala. The region also lent its name to the Sea of Galilee (see Luke 5:1, "Lake of Gennesaret"). Josephus describes it as being remarkably beautiful, producing abundant varieties of fruits and trees.[160]

Perhaps the disciples were blown off course by the wind, making landing in Bethsaida difficult or undesirable. Perhaps Mark wants the reader to see some significance in this detour. The disciples are unable to go to Bethsaida since they are unable to understand about the loaves (6:52) and do not reach this destination until later (8:22).

**They begged him to let them touch even the edge of his cloak (6:56).** The edge of Jesus' cloak refers to the tassels with a blue cord that the law obliged Jewish males to wear and that was to remind them of the commandments of the Lord (Num. 15:37 – 41; Deut. 22:12). A bundle of dyed unspun wool to make these fringes was found in the caves of Bar Cochba. Some unfinished fringes revealed how they were made.[161]

## Dispute Over Purity Issues (7:1 – 23)

**The Pharisees and all the Jews do not eat unless they give their hands a ceremonial washing (7:3).** The Pharisees

---

### ▸ Purity

The Pharisees' attention to purity derived from God's command for Israel to be a holy people and from the many biblical directives about holiness.[A-20] Purity is important because impurity drives God's presence from the midst of the people and will result in their expulsion from the land (18:24 – 30). Impurity belongs to the realm of death and demons and cuts a person off from God. It clings to a person and can be transferred to other persons, vessels, clothes, and houses by touching, lying, or sitting.[A-21] Serious impurity occurring anywhere among the people pollutes the sanctuary where God dwells (15:31). Impurity is not a sin; it comes naturally in the course of life, but it prevents one from approaching what is holy. What the Pharisees considered sinful was choosing not to avail oneself of the opportunity to be cleansed of the impurity.

The Pharisees clarified purity rules that label persons, objects, and places as pure or polluted and susceptible to impurity. Something becomes "impure" or "dirty" when "it is the wrong *thing* appearing in the wrong *place* at the wrong *time*."[A-22] Interest in purity, therefore, stems from a universal human aversion to dirt, disease, and death and to the desire to keep everything in its proper place. Washing was the normal means of removing most impurity.

The Pharisees sought to promote obedience to God's law among the people and took for granted that true obedience would conform to their particular interpretation of the law. With their purity maps charting what was clean or unclean, permissible or forbidden, the Pharisees strove to impose their vision of what God required on all Israel. Maintaining purity was a key item in their agenda, and they applied to everyone many purity laws meant only for priests serving in the temple. The legislation in Exodus 30:18 – 21 (see 40:12, 31), for example, required priests engaged in the tabernacle service to wash their hands. Nowhere does the Bible stipulate that others must wash their hands for ritual purity.

To understand the Pharisees' concerns, we might apply a variation of the aphorism that a man's home is his castle. The Pharisees believed that a man's home is his temple, and he must apply the purity concerns that in the Scripture only pertained to priests.[A-23] Holiness is not given to priests alone but to priests, Levites, and all Israel.[A-24] Every Israelite must be prepared to come into God's presence.

protest publicly that Jesus' disciples eat with defiled (lit., "common") hands. "Common" is the opposite of "holy, devoted to God." Mark explains further that "unclean hands" refer to "unwashed" hands (7:2) and inserts an explanation about Jewish ritual washings for Gentile readers unfamiliar with these customs (7:3 – 4). The disagreement over washing hands has nothing to do with hygiene but is a matter of purity, the fitness to offer sacrifice or to take part in a meal.

The Old Testament law does not require ordinary meals to be eaten in a state of purity.[162] Only priests eating sacrificial offerings (Lev. 22:3 – 9) and laypersons eating their portion of their fellowship offerings (7:20 – 21) must eat in a state of purity. The Pharisees have broadened the law to include all Jews eating anything at any time.

The Bible also prescribes immersion to cleanse impurity, but the Pharisees innovated with their tradition to meet the needs of the urban Jew in a Hellenistic age. They reduced the biblical requirement of bathing the whole body and laundering clothes to the simple act of washing hands.[163] By contrast, Josephus describes the Essenes as so scrupulous that they would not eat without first immersing their entire bodies in cold water.[164]

**Holding to the tradition of the elders (7:3).** "The tradition of the elders" was unscriptural law based on interpretations that tried to fill the gaps and silences in the regulations found in Scripture. Because they based their decisions on the logical analysis of the explicit and implicit data in Scripture, the Pharisees regarded them as rooted in Scripture and equal in authority.

In the first century, washing hands had become a widespread custom and a sign of piety and fidelity to God. The *Letter of Aristeas*, describing the translation of the Pentateuch into Greek and written no later than the first century B.C., cites the practice: "Following the customs of all the Jews, they washed their hands in the sea in the course of their prayers to God, and then proceeded to the reading and explication of each point."[165] Later rabbinic tradition, which contains the legacy of Pharisaism, insisted that washing hands did have an explicit biblical basis. "When he washes his hands, he should say, 'Blessed is He who has sanctified us with his commandments and commanded us concerning the washing of hands.' "[166] The Pharisees and their spiritual heirs also asserted that God had delivered their tradition to Moses.[167]

**When they come from the marketplace they do not eat unless they wash (7:4).** Presumably, the elders fear some contamination from contact even with fellow Jews who are nonobservant. According to Josephus, the sectarians at Qumran were far more extreme and regarded it necessary to bathe even after touching a junior member as if he were an alien.[168]

**They observe many other traditions, such as the washing of cups, pitchers and kettles (7:4).** The concern for the

**ANCIENT LATRINE**

A Roman-era public facility at Beth Shean.

▼

# ▶ The Purposes of the Tradition of the Elders

The development of "the tradition of the elders" (Mark 7:3) sought to achieve three goals. First, it made the basic requirement that Israel be holy to the Lord something attainable for every Jew in everyday life. The Pharisees never thought that they were voiding the commands of God — only making them applicable. Their tradition sought to provide clear-cut instructions on every aspect of daily life so that Jews could live in accord with God's law.

Second, the tradition of the elders sought to forestall the dominant pagan culture from making inroads into Jewish life (see Lev. 20:1 – 7). The *Letter of Aristeas* exults in the law that "surrounds us with unbroken palisades and iron walls, to prevent our mixing with any of the other peoples in any matter being thus kept pure in body and soul, preserved from false beliefs, and worshiping the only God omnipotent over all creation" (139). The tradition of the elders helped raise the wall even higher. It encouraged the devout to make conscious efforts to set themselves apart from the unwashed hordes destined for destruction. Actions such as immersion and washing hands were tangible, positive gestures that displayed who God's elect were and who would be vindicated at the end of the age. Purity laws were elevated "because they plainly distinguished Israel from non-Israel and defined Israel as physical and dependent on history and genealogy not on a universal, spiritual idea."[A-25]

The outward signs of obedience in Jesus' day, circumcision, keeping the Sabbath, observing food laws and washing hands, became the badges that marked out the elect as those who were "in." The feelings about this issue could be strong. As one rabbi from a later period expressed it, "Whoever eats bread without previously washing the hands is as though he had intercourse with a harlot."[A-26] Another rabbi was placed under the ban for casting doubt on the tradition of the elders concerning the cleansing of hands.[A-27]

Third, the tradition of the elders assumes that God created order and that human affairs prosper only when things are divinely ordered — even when they may seem only to be minor issues. Eleazar's speech to Antiochus Epiphanes explaining his refusal to eat anything unclean, even when he has been brutally tortured and threatened with death, movingly captures this conviction (*4 Macc.* 5:16 – 21):

> We, O Antiochus, who have been persuaded to govern our lives by the divine law, think that there is no compulsion more powerful than our obedience to the law. Therefore we consider that we should not transgress it in any respect. Even if, as you suppose, our law were not truly divine and we had wrongly held it to be divine, not even so would it be right for us to invalidate our reputation for piety. Therefore do not suppose that it would be a petty sin if we were to eat defiling food; to transgress the law in matters either small or great is of equal seriousness, for in either case the law is equally despised.

The tradition tried to be as precise as possible — hence its reputation for hairsplitting. The rules preserved in the Mishnah about washing hands, for example, specified the quantity of water required, the position of the hands, and the type of vessel to be used. Hands were suspected of being generally unclean because they were fidgety and likely to touch something unclean,[A-28] and the rabbis vigorously debated the degree of uncleanness that hands incurred.[A-29] Such regulations may seem inconsequential to us, but they gave a mundane act holy significance and allowed individuals to show devotion to God in deliberate, tangible ways. They also led some to become so painstaking in their obedience to these rules that they neglected the weightier matters of the law (see Matt. 23:23 – 25). In the case Jesus presents, such fastidiousness overrides obedience to God's law.

purity of cooking pots and bowls is found in Zechariah 14:20 – 21:

> On that day HOLY TO THE LORD will be inscribed on the bells of the horses, and the cooking pots in the LORD's house will be like the sacred bowls in front of the altar. Every pot in Jerusalem and Judah will be holy to the LORD Almighty, and all who come to sacrifice will take some of the pots and cook in them.

This text has to do with the temple's becoming a fit place to worship God in the coming new age. The Pharisees extended the concern to all vessels everywhere. One of the largest tractates in the Mishnah, *Kelim* ("Vessels"), has to do with vessels of all kinds and with their susceptibility to uncleanness.

**"Why don't your disciples live according to the tradition of the elders?" (7:5).** In Jesus' day, people viewed a teacher as entirely responsible for the conduct of his disciples.[169] By publicly belittling Jesus' disciples for blatantly failing to observe basic Jewish tradition, his challengers seek to make him lose face. Someone so popular threatens to reduce their sphere of influence when he disregards sacred boundaries carefully erected by their rules and calls into question their role as interpreters. Consequently, they seek ways to smudge his reputation before the crowds. Jesus will not answer insincere questions but instead regains command of the situation with a blistering counterattack.

**Isaiah was right when he prophesied about you hypocrites (7:6).** Hypocrisy is a perceived discrepancy between one's alleged principles and one's behav-

ior. Because the Pharisees so insistently championed strict obedience to the law, they left themselves open to the charge. Hypocrisy can take two forms. A hypocrite may be a play actor who deliberately feigns piety to cloak an inner godlessness; this kind of hypocrite seeks to deceive others. A hypocrite may also be self-deceived; this form of hypocrisy is the more insidious because nothing is easier to prove to oneself than one's own sincerity. Jesus' response shows how those who accuse his disciples of transgressing the tradition of the elders sanction far worse transgressions of the law by means of their traditions.

**Whatever help you might otherwise have received from me is "Corban" (that is, a gift devoted to God) (7:11).** God commands children to honor their parents, and in Jewish tradition that entailed giving them physical necessities.[170]

> Our rabbis taught: What is 'reverence' [for parents] and what is honor? Reverence [refers to one who] does not sit in his parent's place and does not stand in his [parent's] place, he does not contradict his [parent's] opinions, and does not judge [his parent's disputes]. 'Honor' [refers to one who] feeds [his father or mother] and gives him (or her) drink; he clothes him (or her) and covers him (or her), and helps him (or her) to enter and exit.[171]

Jesus gives an extreme example of a son who spitefully or selfishly vows that his property is an offering dedicated to the temple. "Corban" refers to something that is taboo as an offering to God. The property becomes "most sacred" even before it is brought to the temple and bars the one who makes the vow or others who are specified in the vow from gaining profit from it (based on the exegesis of Lev. 6:18; Deut. 26:14). In this case, the son prevents his parents from having any benefit from the property. The term "Corban" also applies to the dedicatory formula used in a vow to set aside property for God.172 As a legal device, it only expresses an intention to give property to God and is not the actual disposal of it. The person could keep the property in his possession but say to his parents that he cannot offer them any help because he has dedicated it to God.

The Pharisees regarded breaking this vow to use the property in any way to help the parents as a grave sin. One example from the Mishnah shows how intricate legal fictions developed around such vows:

> If a man was forbidden by a vow to have any benefit from his fellow, and he had naught to eat, his fellow may give [the food] to another as a gift, and the first is permitted to use it. It once happened that a man at Beth Horon, whose father was forbidden by a vow to have any benefit from him, was giving his son in marriage, and he said to his fellow, "The courtyard and the banquet are given to thee as a gift, but they are thine only that my father may come and eat with us at the banquet." His fellow said, "If they are mine, they are dedicated to Heaven." The other answered, "I did not give thee what is mine that thou shouldst dedicate it to Heaven." His fellow said, "Thou didst give me what is thine only that thou and thy father might eat and drink and be reconciled one with the other, and that the sin should rest on his head!" When the case came before the Sages, they said: Any gift which,

if a man would dedicate it, is not accounted dedicated, is not a [valid] gift.173

In Jesus' example, the command to honor parents (Ex. 20:12; Deut. 5:16) and the command to honor vows (Deut. 23:21 – 23) clash head-on. From his point of view, the command from the Decalogue to honor parents soars above the command to honor vows. The Pharisees' tradition, however, turns the law on its head by insisting that the sanctity of the vow supersedes the parents' right to support. Jesus assumes that such a vow is automatically invalid because it violates God's command to honor parents.

**Nothing outside a man can make him "unclean" by going into him. Rather, it is what comes out of a man that makes him "unclean" (7:15).** Jesus not only disputes the legitimacy of the Pharisees' tradition, he rejects the entire basis of Jewish food laws by proclaiming that contact with supposedly impure things or persons does not defile a person. He illustrates his point with an indelicate reminder of what happens to food when it is consumed. It passes through the digestive tract and winds up in the latrine. He concludes from that process that God only cares about defilement that touches the heart (7:21, 23). The heart is the core of motivation, deliberation, and intention. Food does not enter the heart, and what does not enter the heart cannot make a person unclean. How one handles food is therefore morally irrelevant. Nothing from outside pollutes a person.

Jesus reiterates for emphasis that what comes out of a man is what makes him "unclean" (7:20) and then lists vices that flow from the heart. These cannot be cleansed by a fistful of water in cupped hands. God requires that we scour our hearts. If the only thing that matters to God is what comes from a person's heart, then this opens the door for the recognition that God will accept all persons who cleanse their hearts and exhibit faith. Clean/unclean laws establish boundaries, and the Pharisees set themselves up as the border guards. Jesus breaks down the boundaries and claims that true uncleanness has to do with moral impurity, not ritual impurity.

**(In saying this, Jesus declared all foods "clean") (7:19).** The parenthesis in the NIV text interprets this statement as a narrator's aside drawing the conclusion that Jesus declares all foods clean. The phrase, "In saying this, Jesus declared," is not in the Greek text. Literally, it reads, "cleansing all foods." The nominative participle, "cleansing" would modify the verb "he says" in 7:18.

A variant reading, however, has an accusative singular participle that would modify the noun "latrine" immediately preceding it. If this is the original reading, the statement affirms that the food has become clean in the process of elimination. This reading surprisingly fits the rabbinic laws of clean and unclean. According to the Mishnah, excrement is not ritually impure.[174] Rabbi Jose is said to ask: "Is excrement impure? Is it not for purposes of cleanliness?"[175] Even the excrement of a person suffering an unclean emission is not impure.[176] By contrast, the much stricter Qumran sectarians, under the influence of Deuteronomy 23:12 – 14 and Ezekiel 4:12 – 15, considered it to be impure.[177] This startling judgment may be the key to Jesus' argument. Jesus may not declare all foods clean — although that is a legitimate inference — but with droll humor may be exposing the illogic of the Pharisee's arguments. If food defiles a person, as the Pharisees claim, why do they not regard it as unclean when it winds up in the latrine? Defilement must come from some other source than food. The logic derives from the Pharisees' own rules regarding clean and unclean and sets up his concluding words on the real source of defilement: what comes from the heart.

## The Syrophoenican Woman (7:24 – 30)

**Jesus left that place and went to the vicinity of Tyre (7:24).** After the controversy of 7:1 – 23, Jesus withdraws and seeks to remain incognito. In the Old Testament, Tyre was a godless city, and Josephus identifies the people from Tyre "as our bitterest enemies."[178] People from Tyre and Sidon, however, have already flocked to Jesus, which explains how his fame has preceded him (3:8).

**The woman was a Greek, born in Syrian Phoenicia (7:26).** The Romans distin-

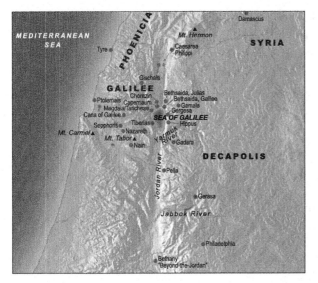

tion explains that "as the sacred food was intended for men, but not for the dogs, the Torah was intended to be given to the Chosen People, but not to the Gentiles."[183] Asenath, after her conversion, took her royal dinner of food that had been sacrificed to idols and threw it out the window, saying, "By no means must my dogs eat from my dinner and from the sacrifice of the idols, but let the strange dogs eat those."[184]

Does Jesus share this Jewish prejudice against Gentiles? There is no indication in the text that Jesus is struggling with the scope of his mission, and this woman helps him to clarify it by opening his eyes to a wider mandate. He has already received people from Tyre and Sidon (3:8).

Jesus may be reacting to a member of the oppressive upper class.[185] Economically, Tyre took bread away from Galilee. This region was well stocked with

◀ *left*

**GALILEE AND PHOENICIA**

Tyre was located on the coast northwest of Galilee.

guished between Lybiophoenicians and Syrophoenicians; this note would seem to reflect a Roman orientation.[179] She is a pagan who comes from a Greek-speaking, more affluent class.

**First let the children eat all they want (7:27).** Israel identified itself as the children of God.[180] A rabbinic tradition expands on Deuteronomy 14:1: "Beloved are Israel, for they were called children of God; still greater was the love in that it was made known to them that they were called children of God, as it is written: Ye are the children of the Lord your God."[181] Jesus' response assumes that Israel has priority in the blessings of the gospel.

**For it is not right to take the children's bread and toss it to their dogs (7:27).** For Israel, "dogs" evoked an image of repulsive scavengers; they will eat anything and never seem satisfied. The word became a term of ultimate scorn and was applied to Gentiles, all of whom were considered to be inherently unclean: "He that separates from the foreskin [Gentile] is as one who separates himself from a grave."[182] Another rabbinic tradi-

◀

**TYRE**

Roman remains in the ancient city of Tyre.

food produced in the Galilean hinterland while Galileans went hungry (see Acts 12:20).[186] Galileans perceived Tyre as a bloated bully and had long despised it for amassing wealth at the expense of the poor.[187] The probing of this woman's faith occurs in the historical context of the animosity between Jews and heathens and Galilean resentment over Tyre's socioeconomic domination.

**But even the dogs under the table eat the children's crumbs (7:28).** This clever woman understands that he is talking about the priority of Israel over Gentiles and that the time for Gentiles has not yet come. But her desperation and faith keep her from taking no for an answer. She comes like a dog begging for a scrap and displays extraordinary faith. She will not be put off by his initial rejection and pleads for help, knowing that she has no merit and nothing to commend her.

### A Deaf Tongue-tied Man Regains His Hearing (7:31 – 37)

**Then Jesus left the vicinity of Tyre and went through Sidon, down to the Sea of Galilee and into the region of the Decapolis (7:31).** Returning from the district of Tyre by way of Sidon to the Sea of Galilee through the district of the Decapolis is a circuitous route. Sidon is twenty-five miles north of Tyre. This indirect route may hint that Jesus was evading the long arm of Herod Antipas. Mark places Jesus in a culturally pagan region.

**After he took him aside, away from the crowd, Jesus put his fingers into the man's ears. Then he spit and touched the man's tongue (7:33).** Healing in the ancient world was a hands-on activity. Healers were expected to do some purposeful action to restore health. Such physical gestures would be particularly important for one who could not hear the spoken words of healing. Putting his fingers in the man's ears was symbolic of opening them and spitting and touching his tongue was symbolic of loosening his tongue. Saliva was also believed to have healing properties.

**He looked up to heaven and with a deep sigh said to him, "Ephphatha!" (which means, "Be opened!") (7:34).** Jesus' healing words in Aramaic are translated to make clear that he is not using some magical incantation. A parallel story about the newly enthroned emperor Vespasian is instructive:

> Vespasian as yet lacked prestige and a certain divinity, so to speak, since he was an unexpected and still new-made emperor; but these were also given to him. A man of the people who was blind, and another who was lame, came to him together as he sat on his tribunal, begging for the help for their disorders which Serapis had promised in a dream; for the god declared that Vespasian would restore the eyes, if he would spit upon them, and give strength to the leg, if he would deign to touch it with his heel.
>
> Though he had hardly any faith that this could possibly succeed, and therefore shrank even from making the attempt, he was at last prevailed upon by his friends and tried both things in public before a large crowd; and with success.[188]

The story reflects the belief that the saliva of a revered person has healing power. In contrast with Vespasian, Jesus does not perform miracles with any hesitancy about his ability or to win prestige.

## The Feeding of Four Thousand (8:1 – 12)

Jesus' compassion prompts him again to feed a large crowd that had been with him for three days without anything to eat (8:2; see 6:34). In this second feeding, the number fed drops from five thousand to four thousand. The loaves and fishes increase from five loaves and two fishes (6:41) to seven loaves and a few small fish (8:5, 7).

**Seven basketfuls (8:8).** The number of baskets of fragments left over diminishes from twelve (6:43) to seven (8:8). The word *kophinoi* (6:43; 8:19) is associated with Jews by Juvenal, but that does not make the common word *spyrides* (8:8; 8:20) into a Gentile basket.[189]

**He got into the boat with his disciples and went to the region of Dalmanutha (8:10).** Jesus sets sail with his disciples to Dalmanutha, a place that is never mentioned elsewhere in ancient literature. The best guess is that it refers to the anchorage of the district of Magdala.

**He sighed deeply and said, "Why does this generation ask for a miraculous sign? I tell you the truth, no sign will be given to it" (8:12).** This generation, represented by the Pharisees, asks Jesus for some apocalyptic sign to signal Israel's final deliverance from her enemies. A sign from heaven is something that "is apocalyptic in tone, triumphalistic in character, and the embodiment of one of the 'mighty deeds of deliverance' that God had worked on Israel's behalf in rescuing it from slavery."[190]

The English translation misses how sharply Jesus refuses. The text reads literally, "If a sign shall be given to this generation." It comprises part of a vehement oath formula that would begin or conclude: "May God strike me down" or "May I be accursed of God" if a sign is given to this generation. Only false prophets will give signs to this generation (13:22, 30).

## The Disciples' Incomprehension (8:13 – 21)

**Watch out for the yeast of the Pharisees and that of Herod (8:15).** "Yeast" connotes to moderns something fresh and wholesome that makes dough rise and gives bread a pleasing light texture. "Leaven," the word used, was far more dangerous. It was produced by keeping back a piece of the previous week's dough, storing it in suitable conditions, and adding juices to promote the process of fermentation, much like sourdough. This homemade rising agent was fraught with health hazards because it could easily become tainted and infect the next batch. In the Old Testament, leaven symbolizes corruption and the infectious power of evil. This image was widely understood. Plutarch wrote that leaven "is itself also the product of corruption, and produces corruption in the dough with which it is mixed . . . and

**MAGDALA**

Magdala was located on the northwest coast of the Sea of Galilee.

▼

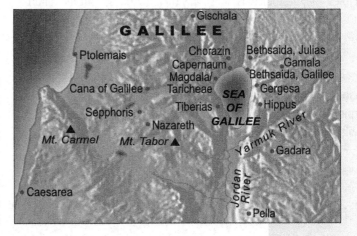

altogether the process of leavening seems to be one of putrefaction; at any rate if it goes too far, it completely sours and spoils the dough."[191]

## Healing a Blind Man (8:22 – 26)

**They came to Bethsaida, and some people brought a blind man and begged Jesus to touch him (8:22).** Bethsaida was reached by sea, not by land, from Capernaum. After refusing to give the Pharisees a sign (8:11 – 13), this healing reveals that Jesus does miracles to meet genuine needs. Dust, poor hygiene, and the bright sun made eye diseases common in the ancient world. Mark describes Jesus taking the blind man away from the village, where he probably had come to beg.

**When he had spit on the man's eyes and put his hands on him (8:23).** Pliny recommends the use of saliva for eye diseases.[192] Jesus' first attempt to heal the man meets with only partial success. This detail communicates two things. First, his blindness is stubborn and hard to cure but Jesus has power to heal even the most difficult cases. Second, on a literary level, curing the stubborn spiritual blindness of the disciples will also take a second touch.

## Announcement of Jesus' Death and Resurrection (8:27 – 9:1)

This passage is the axis on which the two halves of the Gospel turn. The first half reveals Jesus performing mighty works; the second half shows him bound for the cross and crucified in weakness.[193]

**Jesus and his disciples went on to the villages around Caesarea Philippi (8:27).** Caesarea Philippi lay twenty-four miles north of the Sea of Galilee at the southwestern base of Mount Hermon range. It was the capital of Herod Philip's tetrarchy. Jesus may have retreated to the territory of Herod Philip to escape danger from the more threatening Herod Antipas. Originally, the city was called Panion, which refers to a cave sanctuary dedicated to the Greek God Pan, and the cult was still thriving in the first century. Josephus describes the cave as near the source of the river Jordan.[194] Ironically, Peter's confession occurs in the area where Herod the Great built a grand marble temple to honor the emperor[195] and where his heir enlarged the city and renamed it to honor Caesar.[196] It is

---

### REFLECTIONS

**THE PHARISEES AND HEROD HAVE NOTHING IN COM-** mon except their refusal to believe in spite of the evidence. They deny the truth evident in Jesus' ministry. The disciples, too, are in danger of succumbing to the spiritual virus of hardened hearts that causes them to fail to recognize the miraculous truth about Jesus even though they have witnessed his deeds firsthand.

Their failure, before the resurrection, to grasp everything reflects the condition of those governed by the spirit of human wisdom who have not received God's Spirit to reveal God's ways. The disciples are mirror images of modern-day disciples. "The disciples' major problem is not simply their blindness, but the failure to recognize that they are blind."[A-30] We are no less slow-witted or subject to confusion.

The text does its work when readers can see their own blindness in the disciples' blindness. If we ask, "How could the disciples be so dense?" we need immediately to ask the same question of ourselves. The disciples saw dimly in a glass coated with the dust of traditional ways of viewing things and warped by the curvature of their own dreams and ambitions. The glass we look through is no different. We are no less in need of healing before we can see what God is doing, and it may not take on the first try.[A-31]

"theologically significant that Jesus' dignity was recognized in a region devoted to the affirmation that Caesar is lord."[197]

**They replied, "Some say John the Baptist; others say Elijah; and still others, one of the prophets" (8:28).** Popular opinion regards Jesus as some kind of prophet figure (see also 6:14 – 15). Identifying Jesus as a prophet attributes significant status to him and should not be missed. Many Jews in this time believed that the prophetic Spirit had been withdrawn from Israel. In 1 Maccabees 4:41 – 46, Judas Maccabeus has cleansed the sanctuary and torn down the altar defiled by the pagan sacrifices of Antiochus Epiphanes. He stored "the stones in a convenient place on the temple hill until a prophet should come to tell what to do with them" (4:46). The end of 1 Maccabees records the decision that Simon (and the Hasmonean line) should be "their leader and high priest forever, until a trustworthy prophet should arise" (14:41). This view presumes that trustworthy prophets have left the scene, and this prophet is yet to come (Deut. 18:15; Mal. 4:5). Some expected the great prophets such as Isaiah and Jeremiah to return at the end (*5 Ezra* 2:18).

**You are the Christ (8:29).** Under Jesus' interrogation, Peter makes the right confession. By the time of the first century the word Christ (i.e., Messiah) was understood by most Jews to refer to a king-like figure who would triumphantly appear in the final days to deliver Israel from her enemies. The dream did not die even after the debacle with Rome.

Peter's answer is correct since it corresponds to the title of the Gospel (1:1), but Jesus modifies standard expectations by announcing his impending suffering

(8:31). Jesus will not take up the crown but the cross. Suffering, rejection, and death will be God's means of deliverance. Only then will resurrection follow.

**He then began to teach them that the Son of Man must suffer many things . . . , and that he must be killed (8:31).** Mark records three instances when Jesus informs his disciples that the Son of Man must suffer, die, and then be raised (8:31; 9:30 – 31; 10:32 – 34). Significantly, he speaks about this suffering *plainly* (8:32), not in parables (cf. 4:33). Each time, however, the disciples demonstrate in some way that they fail to grasp his meaning. They may have shared the expectations of most Jews, who hoped for a Messiah. He would be a kingly figure who would reign triumphantly as David had (see "Messianic Expectation in Judaism"). No wonder the disciples have trouble assimilating Jesus' announcements about his suffering if they believe he is the Messiah. It runs counter to their every expectation about the Messiah.

**And after three days (8:31).** "After three days" can mean "a short time later." The third day is the time when God has been known to intervene.[198] The intention

**THE JORDAN RIVER AT CAESAREA PHILIPPI**

The waterfall at Banias, near the source of the river.
▼

of this prophetic utterance was not to pinpoint in advance the timing of his resurrection but to certify that it will happen in fulfillment of God's plan. "The full import of the prophecy cannot be grasped until after the event."[199]

**Get behind me, Satan! (8:33).** The archenemy appears in Jesus' most prominent disciple. It is satanic to plot Jesus' death for selfish reasons (3:6, 23 – 26); it is equally satanic to try and block it for selfish reasons (8:33). Ironically, Satan uses one disciple, Peter, to try to turn Jesus away from death, and another disciple, Judas, to lead him to death.

Jesus' stern rebuke is a teaching tool, not a rejection of Peter. In the Qumran literature, chastisement by God was considered to be a requisite for spiritual growth and something for which to be grateful to God.[200] Harsh censure was considered appropriate in the case of recalcitrant students. Philodemus, for example, believed that teachers should use harsh remedies as wise doctors do and show benevolent care by using blame.[201]

**If anyone would come after me, he must deny himself and take up his cross and follow me (8:34).** Jesus does not speak only to the twelve disciples but also to the crowds. He does not want them simply to marvel but to follow him. The cross is a startling image because only criminals and slaves were crucified and carried crosses to the place of execution. Plutarch reports, "Every criminal condemned to death bears his own cross on his back."[202] Dionysius of Halicarnassus gives this account:

> A Roman of some note had handed over a slave to his fellow slaves for them to execute. In order to make the punishment generally known, their master ordered them to drag the condemned man first through the forum and other public places and to scourge him while doing so. . . . The slaves who

---

## ▶ Messianic Expectation in Judaism

Three important texts illustrate the kind of Messiah Jews living at the time of Jesus were looking for. *Psalms of Solomon* 17:21 – 25 expresses the earnest longing for a mighty king to come and reign:

> See, Lord, and raise up for them their king, the son of David, to rule over your servant Israel in the time known to you, O God. Undergird him with the strength to destroy the unrighteous rulers, to purge Jerusalem from gentiles who trample her to destruction; in wisdom and in righteousness to drive out the sinners from the inheritance; to smash the arrogance of sinners like a potter's jar; to shatter all their substance with an iron rod; to destroy the unlawful nations with the word of his mouth; at his warning the nations will flee from his presence;

and he will condemn sinners by the thoughts of their hearts.

The author of *4 Ezra* pictures the Messiah as a lion from the *posterity* of David, who will triumph over the eagle (the Romans). He will judge the world and deliver the faithful remnant of Israel (12:31 – 34).

The *Targum Yerušalmi* to Genesis 49:11 exults:

> "How fine is the King, the Messiah, who will arise from those of the house of Judah! He girds his loins and goes forth and sets up the ranks of battle against his enemies and kills the kings together with their commanders and no king and commander can stand before him. He reddens the mountains with the blood of their slain and his garments are dipped in blood. . . ."[A-32]

had been thus commanded stretched out both the man's arms and tied them down to a piece of wood which reached across breast and shoulders to his wrists. They chased him and lacerated his naked body with their lashes. Overcome by this cruel treatment, the convict not only uttered the most heartrending cries, but under the painful impact of the lashes he also made indecent movements.[203]

Besides the cruel horror of crucifixion, the Jews also believed that anyone who was hanged on a tree was accursed of God (Deut. 21:22 – 23). By inviting followers to take up a cross, Jesus offers them a shameful stigma to go with agonizing suffering.

## The Transfiguration (9:2 – 13)

**After six days Jesus took Peter, James and John with him and led them up a high mountain, where they were all alone (9:2).** "After six days" means that Jesus' transfiguration occurs on the seventh day after Peter's confession. Tradition associates the high mountain with Mount Tabor (1,843 feet), but since a Roman camp was located there[204] and Jesus is still in the region of Caesarea Philippi, it is more likely to be the much higher Mount Hermon (9,166 feet).

**There he was transfigured before them (9:2).** Jewish readers would associate "dazzling white garments" with traditions about the radiant clothing of divine figures (Dan. 7:9) and of the righteous in the resurrection.[205] This event may foreshadow Jesus' resurrection, but Otto concludes: "It is not a vision of *what is to be*, but a revelation of *what already is*, a revelation of the unchanging divine glory which has been concealed beneath the lowliness of a human body."[206] The trans-

figuration is like a hologram that allows disciples to glimpse Jesus' divine glory.

**And there appeared before them Elijah and Moses, who were talking with Jesus (9:4).** Elijah ascended in a whirlwind into heaven (2 Kings 2:11). Later rabbinic interpretations combined the reference to Moses' death, "no one knows . . . his grave" (Deut. 34:6), with the passage "and [he] was there with the LORD" (Ex. 34:28) to conclude that Moses was taken to heaven without death, like Enoch and Elijah. This may have been a popular belief in Jesus' time.[207] Their translation to heaven meant that they were believed able to return to earth. What does their presence signify?

(1) Both were faithful servants who suffered because of their obedience, were rejected by the people of God, and were vindicated by God. The same thing will happen to Jesus.

(2) The people expected a prophet like Moses (Deut. 18:15), Israel's first deliverer, to liberate them once and for all. Elijah was supposed to appear at the dawning of the end time and God's ultimate redemption of Israel. According to *4 Ezra* 6:25 – 26, one of the signs of the end of the age is that those who are left will "see those who were taken up, who

from their birth have not tasted death; and the heart of the earth's inhabitants shall be changed and converted to a different spirit." According to a later rabbinic midrash, God swore to Moses, "in the time to come when I send Elijah, the prophet, unto them [Israel], the two of you shall come together."[208] Their return here denotes the debut of the final age (Deut. 18:15; Mal. 4:5 – 6).

(3) Their presence with Jesus accredits him for his role as the deliverer sent by God. The voice from heaven (9:7) clinches it.

**Peter said to Jesus, "Rabbi, it is good for us to be here. Let us put up three shelters — one for you, one for Moses and one for Elijah" (9:5).** The word translated "shelters" is the word for "tabernacles" or "booths." Otto asks whether this should not be punctuated as a question: "Is it good for us to be here?"[209] This punctuation suggests a measure of fear appropriate to the Sinaitic background of the event and would harmonize with the statement that they were so frightened (9:6).

The *Targum Pseudo-Jonathan* to Exodus 24:10 – 11 develops the account of those who went up the mountain with Moses and saw God. It reads it in light of the declaration that no one will see God and live (Ex. 33:20) and adds that Nadab and Abihu were struck down on the eighth day because they had seen the divine glory. Witnessing Jesus' divine glory would have been terrifying (compare Ex. 19:21) since it could kill those who were unworthy. Peter is a sinner, not a priest, nor is he ritually purified. He does not think it is good to be there in the presence of divine glory; thus he wants to build tabernacles to protect him and the others, physically and psychologically. The tabernacles would veil them from this divine glory radiating from these glorified saints and Jesus.

Otto comments, "The only means by which the people may approach God was through their elect mediator in the *skēnē*, the tabernacle and the tent of meeting, where the power of God's glory was veiled by the cloud."[210] The overshadowing cloud that descends on them signifies the divine glory but also provides them protection. Exodus 19:9 provides the backdrop: "The LORD says to Moses [on Sinai], 'I am going to come to you in a dense cloud, so that the people will hear me speaking with you and will always put their trust in you.'" The command to listen to Jesus means that God is now speaking directly through him.

## Descent From the Mountain (9:9 – 13)

**Jesus gave them orders not to tell anyone what they had seen until the Son of Man had risen from the dead (9:9).** The transfiguration is sandwiched between announcements of Jesus' death. The truth about Jesus' glory can only be fully understood when coupled with his suffering, death, and resurrection. Until that

**GALILEE AND THE NORTH**

Mount Hermon is the likely place of Jesus' transfiguration.
▼

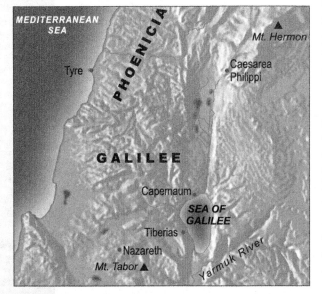

MEDITERRANEAN SEA

PHOENICIA

Mt. Hermon

Tyre

Caesarea Philippi

GALILEE

Capernaum

SEA OF GALILEE

Tiberias

Nazareth

Mt. Tabor ▲

Yarmuk River

takes place, the secret is not yet ready for public proclamation.

They asked him, "Why do the teachers of the law say that Elijah must come first?" (9:11). The teachers of the law based their opinion on Malachi 4:5 – 6 (see Sir. 48:10). Jesus confirms the scribal opinion, but surprisingly asserts that Elijah has already come.

Speculation about Elijah's return and his task of restoration appears to have been diffuse in Judaism. The later rabbis mostly assume that Elijah will solve legal disputes.[211] Others imagine that he will revive the dead, bring back Moses and the desert generation, recover the lost sacred temple vessels, crush mountains like straw, and reveal the great mystery. The disciples' question assumes that some connection between Elijah and the coming of the Messiah existed in Jesus' day, which seems to have faded in later rabbinic literature. Christian literature preserves the conviction that Elijah will identify and anoint the Messiah.[212] Contrary to any current expectation, Jesus announces that Elijah has come and was mistreated.

Jesus rejects any personal identification with Elijah (8:28) and can only have in mind John the Baptizer, who came in the garb of Elijah. Clearly his coming does not herald imminent messianic splendor for Israel. "Restor[ing] all things" has to do with repentance, which was fulfilled when all Judea and Jerusalem came to John to be baptized, confessing their sins (1:5).

## A Father's Plea for His Possessed Son (9:14 – 29)

Jesus returns from the mountain to the everyday world of human and demonic mayhem. The disciples have proven incapable of exorcising a demon, threatening the life of a little boy.

Teacher, I brought you my son, who is possessed by a spirit that has robbed him of speech. Whenever it seizes him, it throws him to the ground. He foams at the mouth, gnashes his teeth and becomes rigid (9:17 – 18). Many have pointed out that the boy's symptoms fit descriptions of epileptic seizures (see Matt. 17:15), but Mark intends to describe the severity of the boy's suffering under the power of an unclean spirit rather than to give evidence for some medical diagnosis. Pilch argues, "The Western tendency to rationalize the ancient understanding of spirits is rooted in the fact that the Westerners have much more power over their lives and circumstances than the ancients believed they had."[213] Attempts to give the boy's self-destructive affliction (Mark 9:22) a modern medical name do not alleviate the evil behind it. Demonic powers always seek to destroy. Josephus comments in an aside that what are called demons "enter the living and kill them unless aid is forthcoming."[214]

The exorcisms in Mark are not simply deeds of kindness and compassion but demonstrations of the divine power and wrath against Satan. In contrast to 5:1 – 13, this exorcism is not a struggle with a demon but a struggle for faith (9:21 – 24). It serves as a concrete example of the truth of Paul's statement that the gospel "is the power of God for the salvation of everyone who believes" (Rom. 1:16).

The spirit shrieked, convulsed him violently and came out. The boy looked so much like a corpse that many said, "He's dead" (9:26). Demons always cause some kind of harm or noise when they exit. The final attack elicits the crowd's skeptical deduction. In 9:27, Jesus takes the boy by the hand (see 1:31; 5:41) and by his power "raises him" (the literal Greek rendering), as it were, from the dead.

**His disciples asked him privately, "Why couldn't we drive it out?" (9:28).** The scene reveals how feeble the disciples are when left to their own devices. In the ancient world, magicians sought to hit the right combination to invoke the power to achieve the desired goals. They weaved esoteric spells using special words, performed unusual actions, and utilized special instruments. Success was all a matter of technique that would force the power to do the bidding of the sorcerer. The disciples' question about what they did wrong verges on this attitude.

**[And fasting] (9:29).** This phrase appears in most of the later New Testament manuscripts but is unlikely to be original. Fasting was an interest of the early church, and the phrase was frequently combined to references to prayer (see its addition to the text in Acts 10:30; 1 Cor. 7:5).[215] Fasting does not fit the context because Jesus has already discouraged fasting as inappropriate until the bridegroom is taken away (Mark 2:18 – 20). He can hardly fault the disciples for failing to do what he has discouraged. He also stresses that the power for exorcism emanates from humble dependence on God, not from some work they perform.

## The Second Announcement of Jesus' Death and Resurrection (9:30 – 37)

**Jesus did not want anyone to know where they were, because he was teaching his disciples (9:30 – 31).** Jesus' public ministry in Galilee is coming to an end, and he desires to spend time teaching his disciples privately, particularly about his suffering and death.

**He took a little child and had him stand among them (9:36).** To squelch the disciples' hankering for worldly greatness, Jesus uses a child as an illustration of kingdom greatness. No romanticized notion of children existed in the first century. Children had no power, status, or rights. They were not considered full persons and were regarded as somewhat akin to property. They were dependent, vulnerable, unlearned, and entirely subject to the authority of the father. The rabbis classified children with the deaf, the dumb, the weak-minded, and slaves. Nowhere else in this period do we find children appealed to as examples to be imitated. To become as a child basically means to recognize one's insignificance. What evokes repentance is the realization that one is as small and slight as a child before God.

### REFLECTIONS

**JESUS' ANSWER REVEALS THAT** prayer is not a magical incantation but a total openness to God's action in and through us. Prayer stops looking to us asking, Why couldn't we drive it out? Disciples do not need to learn better techniques but must make themselves more receptive to the action of God. Since Jesus does not pray before performing the exorcism, prayer is not a one-time invocation of God's power. While special prayers for healing are uttered by Christians (Acts 9:40; 28:8; James 5:15), effective prayer is a continuous posture, not simply an emergency procedure.

## The Strange Exorcist (9:38 – 41)

**Do not stop him (9:39).** Jesus' response to the exorcist who "was not one of us" is similar to Moses' answer when Joshua pled with him to stop unauthorized prophets (Num. 11:26 – 30). Moses responded, "Are you jealous. . . ? Would that all the LORD's people were prophets" (11:29). Disciples are up against hostile forces and will need all the friends they can get. Jesus therefore blesses the humblest act of compassion shown to those who bear his name.

## Temptations to Sin (9:42 – 50)

**It would be better for him to be thrown into the sea with a large millstone tied around his neck (9:42).** A "large millstone" reads literally "a millstone of a donkey," that is, a donkey-powered millstone. This millstone was pierced in the middle to fit a beam attached to a blindfolded donkey, who circled round and round to grind grain or olives.

**If your hand . . . foot . . . eye causes you to sin ( 9:43, 45, 47).** The eye is the cause of covetousness, stinginess, and jealousy. A rabbinic tradition speaks of adultery with the hand (masturbation) and with the foot (a euphemism for the male member), but we cannot limit this passage only to sexual sins.[216] Self-mutilation was prohibited in Judaism, so

Jesus does not intend for one to carry this out literally.[217] He means it is better to accept rigorous discipline now than be punished later.

**Thrown into hell (9:47).** *Gehenna* (translated "hell") derives from the valley of Ben Hinnom outside Jerusalem, where idolaters had once offered child sacrifices.[218] It was later used as a garbage dump, and the burning waste became a vivid image for the place of final punishment.

**Where " 'their worm does not die, and the fire is not quenched' " (9:48).** Jesus quotes the last line of Isaiah (66:24). Worms and fire are images of putrid decay (see Acts 12:23) and flaming destruction (see Rev. 14:11; Judith 16:17), but eternal worms and unquenchable fire (see also Mark 9:43), emitting a noxious stench and an impenetrable column of smoke, refer to everlasting torment. It also means that these sinners will serve as an enduring warning to others of the dangers of sin.

**Everyone will be salted with fire (9:49).** Salt had many functions. It could be used to preserve and purify or to destroy (Judg. 9:45).[219] An early interpretation of this saying appears in a textual variant: "for every sacrifice will be salted with salt" (from Lev. 2:13). The thought may be that disciples are to become sacrifices to God offered up in fiery persecutions. An apocalyptic text reads: "And then all will pass through the blazing river and the unquenchable flame. All the righteous will be saved. But the impious will then be destroyed for all ages. . . ."[220]

**Have salt in yourselves, and be at peace with each other (9:50).** These sayings are parallel. Having salt "among yourselves" means to share salt or eat together (Ezra

◀ *left*

**MILLSTONE**

A large olive press made from basalt found in Galilee at Tabgha.

4:14 [lit. trans.]; Acts 1:4), which is to be done in a spirit of peace.

## Question about Divorce (10:1 – 12)

**Jesus then left that place and went into the region of Judea and across the Jordan (10:1).** "Judea and across the Jordan" reverses the natural geographical order but indicates that Judea is the goal of the journey (see 11:1, where Jerusalem is mentioned before Bethphage and Bethany).

**They said, "Moses permitted a man to write a certificate of divorce and send her away" (10:4).** In biblical times, divorce was not a judgment decided by some court of law. It was an independent action taken by a husband against his wife. The husband's absolute right to divorce his wife was taken for granted by nearly all Jews. According to the rabbis, "The man that divorces is not like the woman that is divorced; for a woman is put away with her consent or without it, but a husband can put away his wife only with his consent."[221] Josephus shares that he divorced his second wife because he was "displeased with her behavior."[222] The husband was only restrained from divorcing his wife if she were insane and unable to care for herself, in captivity,[223] or too young to understand,[224] if he had brought false charges of premarital fornication (Deut. 22:13 – 19) against her, or if he had seduced her and thus had to marry her (22:28 – 29).

Malachi 2:13 – 16 contains the only protest against putting away a wife in the Old Testament, but the Targum to Malachi 2:16 refashions the text to match common practice, rendering it, "If you hate her, divorce her." One rabbi even claimed it was meritorious to divorce a bad wife (citing Prov. 18:22). If her *ketuba*, the sum the husband agreed to pay the wife if he divorced her, was large, he advised marrying another to subject her to the anguish of having a rival.[225]

The instruction given in Deuteronomy 24:1 – 4 was intended to regulate the practice of putting away a wife, not to give the legitimate grounds for divorce. When a husband decided to divorce his wife, the law of Moses required him to give her a bill of divorce and forbad him from ever remarrying her after she became the wife of another man who later divorced her or died. The abomination is not divorce but remarrying the first wife. The law was primarily aimed at preventing this abomination from occurring in Israel.

The Temple Scroll from Qumran envisaged a time when God would renew the people of Israel and the laws concerning divorce, among others, would become passé since there would be no divorce.[226] Jesus' teaching on divorce assumes that this renewal has already dawned.

**But at the beginning of creation God "made them male and female" (10:6).** Jesus asks what Moses *commanded* (10:3) and his opponents respond with what Moses *permitted* (10:4). This response opens the door for Jesus to make his point: Divorce is not a command but a concession because of hardness of heart. The legal stipulations regarding divorce do not mean that God approves of divorce. God's will is to be found in the beginning, in creation. Citing texts combined from the first book of Moses (Gen. 1:27; 2:24), Jesus implies that they contain God's intention for marriage and Moses' real command.

**Anyone who divorces his wife and marries another woman commits adultery against her (10:11).** Jesus contends that marriage is not simply a legal bond but becomes a blood relationship of two persons joined together by God. In Sirach 25:26, we find the advice that if your wife does not go as you would have her go, you should cut her off from your flesh. Jesus rejects any view that regards the spouse as a superfluous limb that can be easily severed. The one flesh relationship is dissolved only by death.

By definition, adultery was the violation of the marriage of your fellow of the covenant, adulterating his property. A man does not violate his own marriage or commit adultery against his wife but only violates the marriage of another married man. Jesus' radical pronouncement holds the husband guilty of adultery against his wife for remarrying.

**If she divorces her husband and marries another man, she commits adultery (10:12).** Only Mark's account of Jesus' teaching on divorce reckons with the possibility of a woman initiating divorce. In the Greco-Roman world, wives were allowed to divorce their husbands, but this action was disallowed in Judaism. A wife could only take steps that would induce her husband to divorce her. We find accounts, however, of women from the Jewish upperclass divorcing their husbands. Josephus reports that Salome, the sister of Herod the Great, sent her husband a bill of divorce and self-righteously declares that it "was not in accordance with Jewish law." He goes on to comment, "For it is (only) the man who is permitted by us to do this, and not even a divorced woman may marry again on her own initiative unless her former husband consents."[227] Josephus also reports that Drusilla, the sister of Herod Agrippa (Acts 25:13), "was persuaded

---

▶ ## Certificates of Divorce in Judaism

*Gittin,* a tractate in the Mishnah, is devoted to the legal ins and outs of divorce bills. It outlines the procedures to be followed in securing witnesses, the contents of the bill, how it is to be delivered (e.g., the husband is not to slip it in her hands at night while she is asleep), and what to do if he should want to withdraw it. The certificate of divorce meant that the husband gave up his right to his wife. It basically said: "Lo, thou art free to marry any man."[A-33] This certificate allowed her to remarry without fear of being accused of adultery or of being reclaimed by her former husband.

The marriage contract was vital because it specified the amount of money she was to receive if

she were divorced or if her husband died. A copy of one belonging to a woman named Babata was uncovered in the Bar Cochba caves. The document was specially wrapped among bundles of others that she kept in a leather purse. It reads, "If I go to my resting place before you, you shall dwell in my house and receive maintenance from it and from my possessions, until such time as my heirs choose to pay you your *Kethuba* money."[A-34] Yadin speculates that she "spent most of her life in litigation, either suing the guardians of her fatherless son or being sued by the various members of her deceased husbands' families."[A-35]

to transgress the ancestral laws" by leaving her husband to marry the Roman governor, Felix.[228] Josephus describes Herodias, who left her husband to marry Herod Antipas, as "taking into her head to flout the ways of our fathers."[229] Jesus may be alluding to this case here.

## Bringing Children to Jesus (10:13 – 16)

**People were bringing little children to Jesus to have him touch them (10:13).** Infant mortality was high in this time. Six of every ten children died before the age of sixteen. "The picture is one of peasant women, many of whose babies would be dead within their first year, fearfully holding them out for Jesus to touch."[230] These parents come from outside the circles of the disciples, and they hope his touch will protect their children from evil. Jesus' loving response reveals that the new community he founds embraces little ones.

## The Rich Man (10:17 – 31)

**"Why do you call me good?" Jesus answered. "No one is good — except God alone (10:18).** Jesus responds sharply to the man's deference. Malina and Rohrbaugh contend concerning this culture:

> Compliments conceal envy, not unlike the evil eye. Jesus must fend off the aggressive accusation by denying any special quality of the sort that might give offense to others. Such a procedure is fully in line with the canons of honor. The honorable person, when challenged, pushes away the challenge and diffuses any accusations that might fuel the position of his opponents.[231]

The man may be implying that while Jesus is a good teacher, he is a good man and should have as great a reputation as he has.

**Go, sell everything you have and give to the poor, and you will have treasure in heaven. Then come, follow me (10:21).** At Qumran, members were required to contribute all their wealth to the common treasury (see also Acts 4:32 – 37; 5:1 – 11). The rabbis, however, forbad giving away one's property. They limited giving to no more than 20 percent to prevent one from being reduced to poverty by excessive generosity.[232]

But this man is identified as a rich man (10:22 – 23). The average peasant assumed that the rich had defrauded others by taking more than their fair share of a limited pie.[233] In the New Testament, the rich are condemned as those who oppress the poor (James 2:6), plunder the property of helpless widows (Mark 12:40; Luke 20:47), and defraud their laborers (James 5:1 – 6). They live in incredible luxury and fare sumptuously (Mark 6:17 – 23; Luke 16:19 – 21) while ignoring the abject poverty of those at their doorstep. They built up surpluses only for themselves, disregarding the disastrous consequences for the rest of society (Luke 12:13 – 21).

When we read "rich" in the New Testament, we should understand it to mean the greedy, dishonorable rich, unless they act in notably charitable ways (see Matt. 27:57 – 60). Therefore, when Jesus asks this man to sell all that he has and give to the destitute, he is simply asking him to redistribute his wealth among those who lack the necessities of life because their portion has been snatched from them. He will simply be returning to them their share. Almsgiving was also associated with true conversion (see Luke 19:8).[234]

**It is easier for a camel to go through the eye of a needle than for a rich man to enter the kingdom of God (10:25).** Jesus uses a deliberately absurd image.

The opening of a needle was the smallest thing imaginable, and the camel was the largest animal in Palestine (cf. Matt. 23:24, where camels are contrasted with gnats). A rabbinic tradition from the Babylonian Talmud remarks that dreams are a reflection of man's thought: "This is proven by the fact that a man is never shown in a dream a date palm of gold or an elephant going through the eye of a needle."[235] The elephant was the largest animal in Mesopotamia, where this tradition was compiled.

Interpretations that try to reduce the size of the camel or enlarge the needle's eye are suspect. There is no basis for the widely circulated tradition that the eye of the needle was the name of a gate in Jerusalem. Walled cities had smaller gates beside or built into a larger gate so that people could enter when the larger gate was closed. Large animals might be able to squeeze through such a gate. Theophylact (eleventh century) seems to have been the first to make this suggestion.[236] Luke uses a different word in Greek for "needle" (*belonē*, Luke 18:25) than Mark (*raphis*). If a gate had been known as "The Needle's Eye," it seems likely that only one Greek term would have been used. Also to be rejected is the textual variant in a couple ancient versions that have the similar sounding *kamilos*, meaning a rope or ship's cable, instead of camel (*kamēlos*). The disciples' shocked response (Mark 10:24a, 26a) reveals that they understand Jesus' statement to be extreme.

Jesus clearly rejects the presumption that prosperity equals divine blessing.[237] His pronouncement recalls the danger of the deceit of riches choking the seed (4:19) and makes clear that salvation is only a divine possibility. It does not mean, however, that wealth is the only obstacle to salvation.

## Jesus' Third Announcement of His Death and Resurrection (10:32 – 45)

**They were on their way up to Jerusalem (10:32).** Regardless of the direction from which one came, one always "went up" to the holy city. Jesus leads the way to his Passion, as he will later lead the way to Galilee after the resurrection (14:28; 16:7).

**Let one of us sit at your right and the other at your left in your glory (10:37).** The disciples recognize that Jesus is destined for great power and ask for special distinction in his messianic kingdom. When Vitellius accepted the title of emperor in A.D. 68, he praised his generals and "placed them on either side of his curule chair."[238] According to the *Psalms of Solomon* 17:26, the Messiah will judge the tribes of Israel, and the disciples may be bidding to share in this messianic authority. Jesus censures the sinful human craving for positions of honor above others.

**Can you drink the cup I drink or be baptized with the baptism I am baptized with? (10:38).** The cup is the cup of suffering from divine judgment.[239] Baptism paints an image of being submerged in suffering (Ps. 42:7; 69:1). The disciples, however, will sleep as Jesus confronts alone in prayer the cup of his bitter destiny (Mark 14:36 – 41).

**Whoever wants to be first must be slave of all (10:44).** The years have dulled the shocking nature of this statement. Plato has Callicles ask: "How can anyone be happy when he is the slave of anyone else at all?"[240] The slave experienced "civil death" with no legal or human rights. Seneca characterizes a slave as one who "does not have the right to refuse."[241] The slave's entire life was at the disposal of the master.

**For even the Son of Man did not come to be served, but to serve, and to give his life as a ransom for many (10:45).** To ransom someone or something means to pay a price to secure its freedom, but it is also a biblical image for the redemption of God's people.[242] Isaiah speaks of making the life of the Suffering Servant "a guilt offering," which brings forgiveness for the lives of the many.[243] In *4 Maccabees* 6:28 – 29 and 17:20 – 22, the death of martyrs is understood to afford vicarious atonement for the people. The difference from Jesus' statement here is that it understands the martyr's death as providing victory over an evil tyrant, whereas Jesus' death offers final deliverance from all evil.

Malina and Rohrbaugh point out that only one of supreme honor could ransom a great number of others who collectively have less honor. Though the king might be just one person, he is worth a whole kingdom of other individuals.[244]

**JUDEA**

The route from Jericho to Jerusalem.

▼

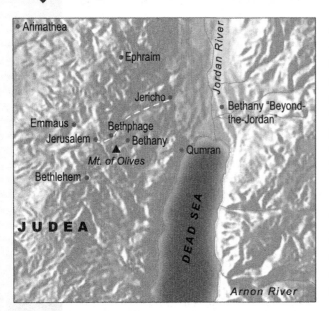

The word "many" may suggest an elite number — many but not all. The "many," however, is a Semitism for "all" (see Mark 1:34; Rom. 5:15, 19). They stand over against the one Son of Man, who acts on their behalf.

## Blind Bartimaeus (10:46 – 52)

**Then they came to Jericho (10:46).** Galilean Jews on pilgrimage to Jerusalem took a detour around Samaria by passing through Perea on the east side of the Jordan. Coming to Jericho, they would make the journey's final leg up the steep road to Jerusalem.

**A blind man, Bartimaeus (that is, the Son of Timaeus), was sitting by the roadside begging (10:46).** Bartimaeus camps along this road to beg alms of the pilgrims. As a blind man, he is not only impoverished but also excluded from participation in the temple worship.[245] A text from Qumran even excludes the blind from the messianic banquet.[246] Since there were so many blind persons in this world, the crowds have become inured to their plight.

**Jesus, Son of David, have mercy on me! (10:47).** The title "Son of David" appears only here in Mark. In this context, it does not have the nationalistic and militaristic connotation normally associated with the term (see *Pss. Sol.* 17). It affirms Jesus' royal authority "expressed in therapeutic works of mercy and deliverance."[247] The healing is linked to another Isaian theme (Isa. 35:1 – 7; 42:16).

**Throwing his cloak aside, he jumped to his feet and came to Jesus (10:50).** The cloak was placed before him to collect alms. It may be his sole worldly possession.[248] He abandons it to come to Jesus.

Rabbi, I want to see (10:51). He addresses Jesus as *Rabbouni* in the Greek (see John 20:16). This means "My dear Rabbi" and expresses more reverent homage than simply "Rabbi" (see Mark 9:5).

## Entry into Jerusalem (11:1 – 11)

**As they approached Jerusalem and came to Bethphage and Bethany at the Mount of Olives (11:1).** Bethphage (meaning "house of early figs") is located closer to Jerusalem than Bethany and is near the summit of the Mount of Olives. Bethany is on the southeastern slopes of the Mount of Olives.

**You will find a colt tied there, which no one has ever ridden. Untie it and bring it here (11:2).** Jesus has walked everywhere else in his ministry except when he crossed the lake in a boat. Riding a colt on this last stage of his journey becomes an enacted symbol that communicates forcefully and dramatically that Jesus is the king of Israel. (1) He impresses the animal as a king would. "The Lord needs it" is the same phrase used to justify David's eating of the bread of the Presence (cf. 2:25). (2) He

impresses the use of a young donkey that has never been ridden. This fits a royal motif. It is an animal suitable for a sacred purpose and worthy of a king.[249] According to the Mishnah, no one else may ride a king's horse.[250] (3) The disciples saddle it with their own garments. When Jehu is anointed king, every man took his garment, put it under him on the steps, and proclaimed, "Jehu is king" (2 Kings 9:12 – 13). This entry into the city may have fueled the charge brought against Jesus to Pilate that he was king of the Jews (Mark 15:2).

A donkey would be apt for a king, but Mark does not identify the animal. Riding "a colt" may express humility. This idea is drawn from Zechariah 9:9, though Mark makes no explicit reference to this verse. He does use the word for the donkey's foal that appears in the

◀

**BETHANY**

*(left)* The location of the ancient road from Bethany to Bethphage. *(right)* The countryside near Jerusalem.

▼

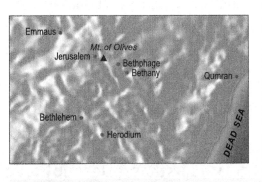

LXX version of Zechariah 9:9. A later rabbinic tradition interprets Daniel 7:13 and Zechariah 9:9 to mean that if Israel is worthy, the Messiah will come upon the clouds; and if not, he will come on a donkey.[251] We cannot know if this tradition was current in the first century.

**As they untied it (11:4).** Twice Mark mentions that the colt is bound and must be untied. This factor may purposely link to Genesis 49:10 – 12, where the one to whom the scepter of Judah belongs binds his colt to the choicest branch and washes his garments in wine.

**Others spread branches they had cut in the fields (11:8).** The practice of spreading branches occurred at various festivals — at the Feast of Dedication and the Feast of Tabernacles.[252] It fits the joyous nature of the Passover celebration.

**Hosanna! Blessed is he who comes in the name of the Lord! (11:9).** "Hosanna" is a Greek transliteration of the Hebrew *Hôšî'âh nā'*, which means "save" or "help, please." Jesus' eye-catching entry into Jerusalem parallels other triumphant entries into the city. After Simon destroyed the last shred of opposition to Maccabean rule by capturing the citadel in the city, "the Jews entered it with praise and palm branches, and with harps and cymbals and stringed instruments, and with hymns and songs, because a great enemy had been crushed and removed from Israel" (1 Macc. 13:51). Josephus reports that in the rebellion against the census of Quirinius, Menahem broke into King Herod's armory on Masada and "returned like a veritable king to Jerusalem" and became a leader of the revolution laying siege to the palace.[253] Jesus' entry may have set up expectations of a kingly rule, but his purpose and actions starkly contrast with those of military ambitions.

**Jesus entered Jerusalem and went to the temple. He looked around at everything (11:11).** Jesus' surveying the area and then leaving recalls Malachi's prophecy of the Lord visiting his temple.[254]

Worshipers entered and exited the temple grounds through the Double Gate in the south wall.[255] From a broad plaza one climbed thirty steps that alter-

---

▶ **Josephus Offers a Firsthand Description of the Temple**

All who ever saw our Temple are aware of the general design of the building, and the inviolable barriers which preserved its sanctity. It had four surrounding courts, each with its special statutory restrictions. The outer court was open to all, foreigners included; women during their time of impurity were alone refused admission. To the second court all Jews were admitted, and, when uncontaminated by any defilement, their wives; to the third male Jews, if clean and purified; to the fourth the priests robed in their priestly vestments.

The sanctuary was entered only by the high priests, clad in the raiment peculiar to themselves.

So careful is the provision for all the details of the service that the priests' entry is timed to certain hours. Their duty was to enter in the morning, when the Temple was opened, and to offer the customary sacrifices, and again at mid-day, until the Temple was closed.

One further point: no vessel whatever might be carried into the Temple, the only objects in which were an altar, a table, a censer, and a lampstand, all mentioned in the Law. There was nothing more; no unmentionable mysteries took place, no repast was served within the building.[A-36]

nated between steps and landings to force an unhurried, reverent ascent. The steps are estimated to have been 210 feet wide. The arch and the original lintel of the Double Gate are still intact, though partially concealed by the remains of a tower built by the Crusaders. Inside the vestibule were domes, sixteen feet in diameter, chiseled with beautifully painted floral and geometric designs. One climbed the tunnel passageway and exited in the temple esplanade. The Royal Stoa lay behind.

The Triple Gate was used by priests and to reach the storerooms for the wine, oil, and flour. In between these gates stood a bathhouse for ritual purification and a council house. Three such courts are mentioned in the Mishnah: a court at the gate of the temple mount, at the entrance to the temple court, and in the Chamber of Hewn Stone (*m. Sanh.* 11:2).

## The Temple Incident and the Cursing of the Fig Tree (11:12 – 25)

**Then he said to the tree, "May no one ever eat fruit from you again" (11:14).** Pliny, the Elder, observed, "The fig tree is also the only tree whose leaf forms later than its fruit."[256] Since it sets its fruit before producing leaves, once it has broken into leaf, it should have produced fruit.

Jesus' odd cursing of a fig tree — the only miracle that brings death and not life — becomes an enacted parable. Jeremiah's outburst against the temple provides the backdrop for understanding it. God forbids the prophet to make any intercession for the people (Jer. 7:16) and then says that his "wrath will be poured out on this place, on man and beast, on the trees of the field and on the fruit of the ground, and it will burn and

not be quenched" (7:20). The parable of the tenants of the vineyard makes the same point: The tenants [of the temple] have borne no fruit to give to the owner and are subsequently destroyed.

Fruitfulness was a symbol of Israel's covenant relation to God. At one point, God delighted in Israel because it was like seeing the early fruit on the fig tree (Hos. 9:10). The blighted tree in a land where trees are scarce becomes a symbol of God's judgment.[257] Withered to the roots, there is no hope for this fig tree's renewal.

FIG BRANCH

Jesus . . . began driving out those who were buying and selling there (11:15). Those buying and selling are trafficking in animals for the sacrifices. The priestly aristocracy's wealth and influence are directly attributable to their control of the fiscal affairs of the temple. Since Jesus throws out *both* buyers and sellers, something more than dishonest profiteering provokes him.

Archaeological discoveries suggest that the temple market was inside the Royal Stoa and not spread out all over the so-called court of the Gentiles.[258] The Royal Stoa was at the intersection of the paved streets of Jerusalem. The main street that ran the length of the Tyropoeon Valley headed north along the western wall of the temple was directly accessible via the steps leading down from Robinson's Arch to the markets on the streets below. The main part of the Stoa was a long rectangular Hall of Columns built in the design of a basilica, with 162 columns in four rows stretching the length of the hall. Josephus describes it as "a structure more worthy to be spoken of than any other under the sun."[259] Mazar concludes that the Royal Stoa contained a smaller market that "served primarily for commerce in the cultic provisions for the Temple."[260]

We should not suppose that the changing of money and the selling of sacrificial objects compromised the holiness of the temple. Some kind of market

was necessary for the daily operation of the temple. The biblical requirement of offering unblemished sacrifices to God necessitated having a supply of sacrificial animals on hand, a means of inspecting the animals for disqualifying blemishes, and a monetary exchange for pilgrims. This activity does not take place within the sacred space of the sanctuary.

**He overturned the tables of the money changers (11:15).** Tables were set up in the outer courts three weeks before Passover to receive the annual half-shekel tax required of every Jewish male (Ex. 30:11 – 16).[261] This tax funded the daily sacrifices for the atonement of sin.[262] For a modest commission, money changers exchanged inadmissible local currencies for the sanctioned Tyrian shekel used to pay the tax. Jewish authorities were forbidden to mint silver coins, and they adopted the Tyrian shekel because of its high quality and because it did not flaunt Rome's dominion over Israel. These coins, however, had an image of the god Melkart (Herakles) on the obverse and an eagle with the inscription, "Tyre the holy and inviolable," on the reverse.

**The benches of those selling doves (11:15).** Doves were the staple sacrifice of the poor who could not afford animals for sin offerings (Lev. 5:7). They were also used for the purification of poor women after child birth (12:6, 8; Luke 2:22 – 24), for men and women who had a bodily discharge (Lev. 15:14, 29), and for poor ex-lepers (14:21 – 22). An incident recorded in the Mishnah describes a time when the cost of doves was exorbitant (two golden dinars for a pair of doves). Fearing that the poor would not bring their offerings at these prices, Rabbi Simeon, the son of Gamaliel, gave a ruling that only one offering would suffice for the five that were required. The bottom fell out of the price in one day to half a silver dinar (1 percent of the original cost).263

**He . . . would not allow anyone to carry merchandise through the temple courts (11:16).** This translation is misleading. It is perhaps based on Josephus's report that no one was allowed to carry vessels into the sanctuary264 and a passage from the Mishnah that forbids using the temple as a shortcut.265 The text, however, says that Jesus prevents them from carrying a "*vessel* through the temple."

"Vessel" is used in the LXX for the sacred temple vessels for the bread of the Presence, lamp oil, and incense censers (see Isa. 52:11: "the vessels of the LORD").

The people involved are probably stunned by the power of Jesus' moral indignation. It is a modest clash since it does not spark the intervention of the Roman soldiers, who monitor the crowd from their post above the temple court in the Antonia Fortress (contrast Acts 21:34). Jesus' actions in the temple market, therefore, do not seem to be some attempt to reform the temple practice. Overturning and driving out evoke images of judgment rather than reform. Those involved will soon set right their tables and pick up the scattered money. There is little comparison to what Jesus did and the purification of the temple by Josiah (2 Kings 23) or Judas Maccabeus (1 Macc. 4:36 – 59).

He is not clearing commercial space for prayer. There is no evidence that the outer court was thought of positively as the place where Gentiles could worship. On the contrary, it was thought of as an area beyond which Gentiles could not go. The balustrade surrounding the sanctuary had warning signs cautioning any Gentile against proceeding any further, threatening death to violators (see Acts

**THE ANTONIA FORTRESS**

A model of the Roman fortress showing the temple precincts in the foreground.

▼

21:27 – 30). There was plenty of room for Gentiles to pray in the outer court, and clearing a place for them to pray does not remove the barrier that kept them from the sacred place.

**But you have made it "a den of robbers" (11:17).** This citation from Jeremiah condemns the Jewish leaders for turning God's sanctuary into a sanctuary for bandits. The den was the hideout where robbers retreated after committing their crimes — their place of security and refuge.

**Therefore I tell you, whatever you ask for in prayer (11:24).** The temple was regarded as the place where prayer was particularly effective; thus, when one was not in the temple, one should orient oneself toward it in prayer.[266] This belief is reflected in the high priest's prayer in *3 Maccabees* 2:10: "And because you love the house of Israel, you promised that if we should have reverses and tribulation should overtake us, you would listen to our petition when we come to this place and pray." Lament over the effect of the temple's destruction on Israel's prayer is recorded in the Talmud:

> R. Eleazar said: From the day on which the Temple was destroyed, the gates of prayer have closed, as it says, "Yea, when I cry for help, He shutteth out my prayer" (Lam. 3:8). . . . R. Eleazar also said: Since the day that the Temple was destroyed, a wall of iron divides between Israel and their Father in Heaven; as it says, "And take thou unto thee an iron griddle and set it for a wall of iron between thee and the city" (Ezek. 4:3).[267]

Jesus' statement implies that the effectiveness of prayer has nothing to do

with the temple or its sacrifices. He will later affirm the judgment of a teacher of the law who says that loving your neighbor as yourself "is more important than all burnt offerings and sacrifices" (12:33).

**By what authority are you doing these things? (11:28).** The priestly hierarchy take seriously any threats against the temple. Not only is it the holy place where God dwells, it provides the priestly caste its livelihood and status and has an enormous impact on the whole Jerusalem economy. Josephus reports that prior to the war against Rome, the leading citizens of Jerusalem arrested a coarse peasant named Jesus, son of Ananias. He had pronounced woes day and night against the city, the people, and the sanctuary. After arresting him, the magistrates were still unable to silence him. In hopes of doing away with him once and for all, they brought him before the Roman governor, who judged him to be a maniac and had him flayed to the bone.[268]

**John's baptism — was it from heaven, or from men? Tell me! (11:30).** Answering a question with a counterquestion was a normal debate tactic that changed the power equation. Jesus will answer their question only on his terms — after they answer him. It puts him "in the driver seat."[269] The priests cannot afford to declare John a charlatan and alienate his pious supporters, nor can they openly endorse him and risk accrediting other charismatic prophets who followed after him — like Jesus. The implication is that John was an eschatological prophet whose divine authority had bypassed institutional lines of command, such as the temple hierarchy. The same holds true for Jesus. His action in the temple is that of a prophet directed by God and not a conventicle of priests and teachers of the law.

## The Parable of the Tenants (12:1 – 12)

**He put a wall around it, dug a pit for the winepress and built a watchtower (12:1).** Stone walls were erected around vineyards to keep out animals and foragers. The towers provided some shelter and a lookout during the grape harvest. The description of the vineyard has striking parallels to Isaiah 5:2 (LXX). Since the hedge, winepress, and tower have no significance in the later development of the story, these details are only included to recall the context in Isaiah that pictures God's lavishing care on the vineyard, his people, but meeting only with ingratitude and unfruitfulness (5:1 – 7). Jesus' parable is thus an allegory of God's troubled relationship with Israel. A fragment from Qumran has been interpreted as applying Isaiah 5 to the temple.[270] The problem is not a vineyard that yields bad fruit, but tenants who yield no fruit.

**Then he rented the vineyard to some farmers and went away on a journey (12:1).** The parable reflects the real world of absentee landlords. Resentment against them was typical, but few would ever dare to behave as the parable's tenants did.[271] In Longus's novel, *Daphnis and Chloe* (4.1 – 14), the master plans to visit the estate where the hero and heroine keep sheep. They work hard to make things as presentable as possible. Daphnis is uneasy about seeing the master who heretofore has been only a name and referred to as the dreaded master. They panic when an enemy vandalizes their garden, assume the master will have them hanged, and pray that he will never come. Then news comes by messenger that their master will arrive in three days but that his son is coming first and will be there the next day. All goes well as Daphnis is commended to the master for doubling his flock.

**Then he sent another servant to them (12:4).** The word "servant" is a transparent metaphor for the prophets since the Old Testament uses it frequently to describe them.[272] God continually sent prophets to Israel (Jer. 7:25 – 26). Persistent mistreatment of them was proverbial.[273]

**They will respect my son (12:6).** Some interpreters debate whether the word

"son" would have been interpreted messianically in the first century. Evidence from the Dead Sea Scrolls referring to the Son of God and Son of the Most High lends credence to the probability that "son" would have been understood in a messianic sense by the audience.[274]

**This is the heir. Come, let's kill him, and the inheritance will be ours (12:7).** The son is on a different level than the servants and crucial for a case involving the disputed ownership of a vineyard. The phrase "Come let us kill him" is the same phrase used by Joseph's brothers in Genesis 37:20a (LXX). It serves to heighten the tenants' guilt, which is compounded by their failure to give the body a burial. To be refused honorable burial is a powerful image of humiliating punishment in Scripture.[275]

**The stone the builders rejected has become the capstone (12:10).** A portion of Psalm 118 was chanted to greet Jesus as he entered Jerusalem (Mark 11:9 – 10/ Ps. 118:25). It is now invoked to explain that the one who is rejected will be vindicated (Ps. 118:22 – 23). The block of stone that the builders rejected becomes the keystone — the wedge-shaped stone placed in the top of an arch that locks the others into position. It is the head of the new structure. An Aramaic play on words between "son" (*ben*) and "stone" (*'eben*) may lie behind this saying.

## Taxes to Caesar (12:13 – 18)

**Pharisees and Herodians (12:13).** See comments on 3:6.

**Is it right to pay taxes to Caesar or not? (12:14).** Judea became a Roman province in A.D. 6 and was subject to the poll tax (or head tax, distinct from the tax on property and customs on articles). The census provided the data (computed in acres and human heads) from which the Romans levied this tax. Its establishment provoked the revolt of Judas of Galilee because it placed God's own land at the service of foreigners.[276] A "yes" answer to Jesus' question invites the charge of turning traitor to God by endorsing Caesar's hegemony over the land. It was also an emotionally charged issue since most residents of Palestine knew someone the Romans sold into slavery, executed, or forced off their land by the whirlpool of debt from the spiraling tax burden. A "no" answer, by contrast, invites the charge of sedition.

**Bring me a denarius and let me look at it (12:15).** By asking for a denarius that he does not possess, Jesus throws them off their guard. In this era, coins served propaganda purposes. Assuming that they show him a Tiberian denarius, the obverse side bore the image of the emperor with the superscription: "TI[berius] CAESAR DIVI AVG[usti] AVGVSTVS." The reverse had a female

right ▶

**COINS**

*(top)* Silver denarius with a portrait of the Roman emperor Tiberius (A.D. 14 – 37).

*(bottom)* A coin depicting the emperor Nero (A.D. 54 – 68).

figure facing right, seated on a throne, with a crown and holding a scepter in the right hand and a palm or olive branch in the left. The superscription reads: "Pontif[ex] Maxim[us]." The Pharisees and Herodians possess a coin oozing idolatry and blasphemy. It touts Tiberius as a divine or semidivine being as the son of the divine Augustus. The woman is a priestess or the wife of Augustus, Livia, proclaiming the *Pax Romana* that places all peoples in subjection.[277]

**Give to Caesar what is Caesar's and to God what is God's (12:17).** This statement places a limit on Caesar's authority. Those things stamped with Caesar's image, such as mere coins, belong to him. Those things stamped with God's image, such as human beings, belong to God. The image that humans are a coin stamped by God's seal is found in a discussion about idolatry and immorality in the Talmud. Sinful humans misuse the sexual instinct God gives them, resulting in the conception of illegitimate children. God complains about this, "Not enough that the wicked put My coinage to vulgar use, but they trouble Me to set My seal thereon!"[278]

## The Question about the Resurrection (12:18 – 27)

**Then the Sadducees, who say there is no resurrection (12:18).** The Sadducees considered the Mosaic directives alone as binding and rejected what they perceived to be theological innovations. Consequently, they did not believe in a resurrection since it does not appear in the Pentateuch.[279] Their attitude may be captured in the hymn to honor ancestors in Sirach 44:1 – 23: The only immortality one can hope for is having posterity and being remembered.[280]

**When the dead rise, they will neither marry nor be given in marriage; they will be like the angels in heaven (12:25).** The Sadducees understand resurrection to be only reanimation. Jesus declares that life in heaven should not be confused with life on earth. He compares it to the life of angels, who are immortal, making procreation and therefore marriage unnecessary.

**Have you not read in the book of Moses, in the account of the bush (12:26).** The reference to the "bush" passage reflects how Scripture was cited before chapter and verse divisions. The point is that the living God will not tie his name to three corpses.

## The Question about the Great Commandment (12:28 – 34)

**Of all the commandments, which is the most important? (12:28).** One rabbi declared that of the 613 commandments given to Moses, 365 were negative precepts, "corresponding to the number of solar days," and 248 were positive commandments, "corresponding to the number of members of a man's body."[281] The Talmud passage goes on to claim that David reduced them to eleven essential principles, Isaiah to six, Micah to three, and Isaiah, again, to two, and Amos to one.[282] This discussion reflects the debate over the relative weight of the various commandments. The rabbis divided them up into light and heavy commandments according to three varying criteria: how severe the penalty was for failing to obey them, how great or little the reward for obeying them, or how easy or difficult they were to fulfill.[283]

**Hear, O Israel . . . (12:29).** Jesus identifies as absolute the first line in the Shema (Deut. 6:4), recited morning and evening by devout Jews, which commands exclusive love for God. He adds a second that is on the same order, love of one's neighbor. Since love is something that is commanded, it has to do with actions rather than feelings.

**Well said, teacher (12:32).** The teacher of the law assumes he is in a superior position and able to pass judgments on Jesus' teaching. Jesus, however, is the final arbiter of the law and of who is near or far from the kingdom of God, and he regains mastery by commending his response.

## Jesus' Question about David's Son (12:35 – 37)

Psalm 110 was assumed to refer to a Davidic figure who would reign with God's authority and crush Israel's enemies. Jesus challenges the views about this abstract figure. Sons may address their fathers as "Lord," but never vice versa. Therefore, Jesus uses the psalmist's words to pose a conundrum about himself as the Son of David (Mark 10:47, 48; 11:10).

## The Denunciation of the Scribes (12:38 – 40)

**Teachers of the law (12:38).** See "Scribes / Teachers of the Law" at 2:7.

**They like to walk around in flowing robes (12:38).** Jesus attacks the human fondness to seek honor, to parade one's caste, and to call attention to one's piety. The long robes refer to the distinctive white linen robes that set them apart from others. They also expect others to show them the greatest respect and greet them as "Rabbi," "Father," "Master" (Matt. 23:7 – 9), or "Good teacher" (Mark 10:17) and to offer them the seats of honor.

**They devour widows' houses (12:40).** Widows are a traditional symbol of the helpless in the Old Testament. Widows without male offspring to protect them were particularly vulnerable, and abusing them is sternly denounced in the Old Testament.[284]

## The Widow's Offering (12:41 – 44)

**Jesus sat down opposite the place where the offerings were put and watched the crowd putting their money into the temple treasury (12:41).** Jesus' presence in the temple began with his condemnation of the buyers and sellers for the animal sacrifices and ends with his commendation of one who sacrifices her all for God. "Opposite the place where the offerings were put" may refer to a special room in the temple or to one of thirteen chests, shaped like a trumpet, that stood around the Court of Women. The verb translated "putting" is the verb "to throw" and suggests throwing something into a chest. The Mishnah mentions shofar-chests labeled for different types of offerings: "new shekel dues," "old shekel dues" (paid only by males), "bird offerings" (for the purchase of turtle doves), "young birds for whole offerings" (for the purchase

of pigeons), "wood" (for burning on the altar), "frankincense," and "gold for the mercy seat"; six were designated "freewill offerings."[285] The small amount of the widow's contribution means that her gift can only go to the freewill offering, which goes to the building of the temple (see Ex. 35 – 36; 1 Chron. 29), or burnt offerings, from which the priests receive the hides.[286]

**But a poor widow came and put in two very small copper coins, worth only a fraction of a penny (12:42).** A widow is indeed poor if she has only two *lepta.* The *lepton* was a tiny copper coin with the least value of any in circulation in the time of Jesus, about one-eighth of a Roman *assarion.* The two *lepta* are said to be worth a *quadrans,* the smallest Roman coin. Four *quadrans* equal an *assarion* which was worth one-sixteenth of a *denarius.* If a day laborer earned a *denarius* for a day's wage (Matt. 20:2), this woman has one-sixty-fourth of that wage. If this is all she has to live on, she is indeed destitute.

A similar story occurs in later rabbinic literature:

> Once a woman brought a handful of fine flour [for a meal offering, Lev. 11:2], and the priest despised her, saying: "See what she offers! What is there to eat? What is there to offer up?" It was shown to him in a dream: "Do not despise her! It is regarded as if she had sacrificed her own life."[287]

Jesus does not need a dream vision to recognize the worth of her extraordinary sacrificial giving.

## The Olivet Discourse (13:1 – 37)

**As he was leaving the temple, one of his disciples said to him, "Look, Teacher!**

**What massive stones! What magnificent buildings!" (13:1).** The highest walls of the temple mount reached 165 feet. Philo reports that Marcus Agrippa, the grandfather of the emperor Gaius (Caligula), visited Jerusalem and could talk of nothing else "but praise for the sanctuary and all that pertained to it."[288] The wonderful buildings elicited pride and a sense of security because of the conviction that the temple was the place where God dwelt: "This is my resting place for ever" (Ps. 132:14). What the disciples did not see was that this temple was like a barren fig tree.

**Not one stone here will be left on another; every one will be thrown down (13:2).** We get a glimpse of the devastation wrought by the Roman army's destruction of the temple in A.D. 70 from the imprint of arches burnt into the bedrock foundations of chambers adjoining the southern retaining wall, east of the Triple Gate. The Ritmeyers explain:

> The limestone ashlars used in the Herodian construction can be reduced to powder when exposed to very high temperatures. The Roman soldiers must have put brushwood inside the chambers and the blaze created when

# HEROD'S TEMPLE

## 20 B.C. – A.D. 70
## Aerial view showing outer courts

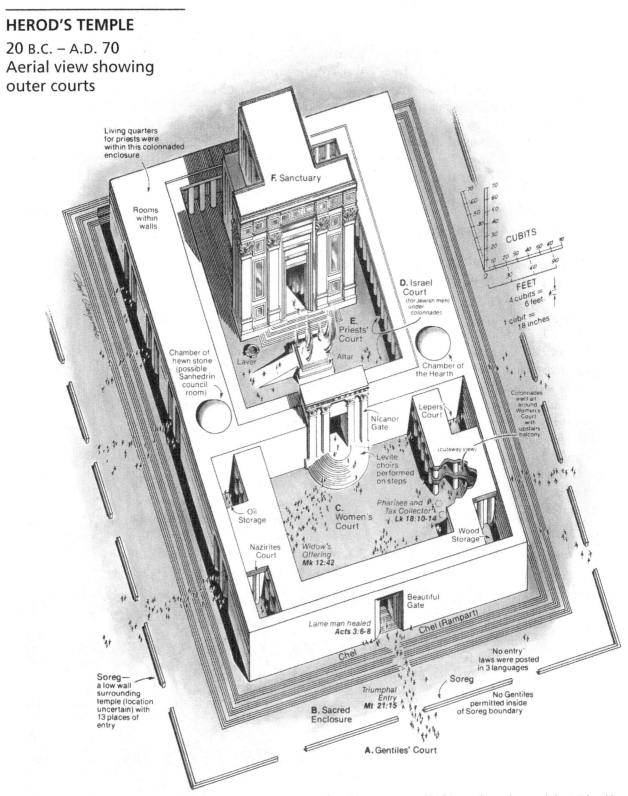

Living quarters for priests were within this colonnaded enclosure

Rooms within walls

**F.** Sanctuary

**D.** Israel Court *(for Jewish men) under colonnades*

**E.** Priests' Court

Chamber of hewn stone (possible Sanhedrin council room)

Laver

Altar

Chamber of the Hearth

CUBITS

FEET

4 cubits = 6 feet

1 cubit = 18 inches

Lepers' Court

Colonnades went all around Women's Court with upstairs balcony

Nicanor Gate

*(cutaway view)*

Levite choirs performed on steps

Oil Storage

**C.** Women's Court

*Pharisee and Tax Collector* ↓ **Lk 18:10-14**

Wood Storage

Nazirites Court

*Widow's Offering* **Mk 12:42**

Beautiful Gate

*Lame man healed* **Acts 3:6-8**

Chel (Rampart)

Chel

Soreg — a low wall surrounding temple (location uncertain) with 13 places of entry

"No entry" laws were posted in 3 languages

Soreg

*Triumphal Entry* **Mt 21:15**

No Gentiles permitted inside of Soreg boundary

**B.** Sacred Enclosure

**A.** Gentiles' Court

Dimensions are stated in history (Josephus and the Mishnah) but are subject to interpretation, and all drawings vary.

this was set alight would have caused the arches to collapse. The street that was carried by these arches also collapsed. Before the arches collapsed, the fire burnt into the back wall of the chambers, leaving the imprint of the arches as evocative testimony to the dreadful inferno.[289]

**As Jesus was sitting on the Mount of Olives opposite the temple (13:3).** According to Ezekiel 11:23, the glory of the Lord retreats from a corrupt Jerusalem to the Mount of Olives (see Zech. 14:4). The Mount of Olives was severely deforested by the Romans during their siege of Jerusalem.[290] In Jesus' day, its groves of pines and olives offered pleasant seclusion.

**Many will come in my name, claiming, "I am he," and will deceive many (13:6).** Jesus warns of a procession of impostors to come (see also 13:21 – 22). Josephus claimed that what incited the nation to war against Rome more than anything else was "an ambiguous oracle" found "in their sacred scriptures, to the effect that one from their country would become ruler of the world."[291] He himself concluded

◀

**"MASSIVE STONES" OF THE TEMPLE**

The western wall ("the wailing wall") of the temple with massive stones from the platform of the Herodian temple.

## ▶ Josephus on the Magnificence of the Temple

With pride Josephus describes the former glory of the temple:

> Now the exterior of the building wanted nothing that could astound either mind or eye. For, being covered on all sides with massive plates of gold, the sun was no sooner up than it radiated so fiery a flash that persons straining to look at it were compelled to avert their eyes as from solar rays. To approaching strangers it appeared from a distance like a snow-clad mountain; for all that was not overlaid with gold was of purest white. . . . Some of the stones in the building were forty-five cubits in length, five in height and six in breadth.[A-37]

## REFLECTIONS

**JESUS DOES NOT ANSWER THE** disciples' questions about the signs and timing of the consummation of the age, but gives instructions on how to discern false signs, punctuated by warnings not to be fooled. The emphasis does not fall on what to know but on how to know. Geddert concludes, "The disciple is not called to eliminate his ignorance of the timing of the End, he is called to cope with it, and respond to it appropriately."[A-38]

Jesus warns that God's cause will meet with greater and greater resistance from the powers of evil until the end. "The eschatological drama will run its course, scene by scene. But the actors on the stage have only vague clues about where they are precisely in the play. Only the stage director knows. He has given the actors instructions about what to do and what to say when they see certain things happen. But that is it. They know how the play ends, but they do not know when the curtain will fall."[A-39]

**MASADA**

Roman ramp built up for the assault on Masada in A.D. 70.

▼

that it referred not to some Jewish leader but to the Roman general Vespasian and castigates those whom he claimed were worse than the violent revolutionaries:

> Another group of scoundrels, in act less criminal but in intention more evil. . . . Cheats and deceivers, claiming inspiration, they schemed to bring about revolutionary changes by inducing the mob to act as if possessed and by leading them out into the wild country on the pretence that there God would give them signs of approaching freedom.[292]

In the second century, Simon was designated the Messiah by R. Akiba, who dubbed him Bar Cochba, "son of the star." After his defeat, later rabbis called him Bar Cosiba, "son of the lie."

**When you hear of wars and rumors of wars, do not be alarmed. Such things must happen, but the end is still to come (13:7).** Jesus' warning is exactly the opposite of what is found in *4 Ezra* 9:1 – 6. In that text, "earthquakes, tumult of peoples, intrigues of nations, wavering of leaders, confusion of princes" are signs of the end. Jesus says that such things are *not* true signs of the end, and they should not cause panic when they occur. They are to be expected along with the persecution that will inevitably befall his followers (13:9 – 11).

**When you see "the abomination that causes desolation" standing where it does not belong (13:14).** "Abomination" refers to what is detestable and rejected by God. It is either an abomination (filth) that causes horror (such as pagan idols, Deut. 29:17) or an appalling sacrilege that makes desolate.[293] The warning relates to events surrounding the destruction of Jerusalem. It will be useless to flee to some mountain refuge at the end of the ages. Those who do will have no time to retrieve precious possessions, even essentials, such as cloaks.

If the abomination refers to something before the Jewish revolt, Gaius Caligula commanded that his statue be erected in the temple. Petronius, the legate of Syria, however, stalled in carrying out the order, and Gaius's assassination prevented a confrontation.[294] If it refers to something during the revolt, the Zealots who occupied the temple precincts committed multiple sacrileges.[295] If it refers to something after the revolt, Josephus reports that after the Romans captured Jerusalem, the soldiers set up their standards in the temple and sacrificed to them, and the general Titus stood in the Most Holy Place.[296] But what good will flight do at this point? If it refers to none of these things, it applies to anything or anyone who seeks to usurp God's place, and the flight should be understood metaphorically.[297]

**Let the reader understand (13:14).** This direction may be some kind of interpretive hint for an esoteric reading of Daniel, or it may be an aside for the one who publicly reads Mark's Gospel to the assembly.[298] Today, personal copies of the Bible are widely available, and many read their Bibles privately. This was not the case in Mark's day, an age of limited literacy. His Gospel would have been read publicly.

Note that the "abomination that causes desolation" is a neuter noun. Good grammar requires the participle "standing" also be neuter, but it is masculine. The aside instructs the one reading the Greek text not to correct the masculine participle with a neuter noun out of some mistaken grammatical sensitivity. What Mark has written, he has written deliberately. The masculine participle makes the abomination refer to a person. Best likens it to our modern *sic*, which is placed after a word that seems odd or misspelled: "But when you see that thing, the abomination of desolation, standing where he [*sic*] should not be. . . ."[299]

**Let those who are in Judea flee to the mountains (13:14).** Eusebius reports:

> But before the war, the people of the Church of Jerusalem were bidden in an oracle given by revelation to men worthy of it to depart from the city and to dwell in a city of Perea called Pella. To it those who believed in Christ migrated from Jerusalem. Once the holy men had completely left the Jews and all Judea, the justice of God at last overtook them, since they had committed such transgressions against Christ and all his apostles. Divine justice completely blotted out that impious generation among men.[300]

By contrast, Josephus tells of numerous prophets who deluded the people by encouraging them to wait for God's help and to seek refuge in the supposedly inviolate temple court.[301]

Dio Chrysostom expresses amazement at the Jewish resistance to the very end during the revolt:

> The Jews resisted [Titus] with more ardor than ever, as if it were a kind of windfall [an unexpected piece of luck] to fall fighting against a foe far outnumbering them; they were not overcome until a part of the Temple had caught fire. Then some impaled themselves voluntarily

on the swords of the Romans, others slew each other, others did away with themselves or leaped into the flames. They all believed, especially the last, that it was not a disaster but victory, salvation, and happiness to perish together with the Temple.[302]

**Let no one on the roof of his house go down or enter the house to take anything out (13:15).** Since Palestinian roofs were flat, they served as an extra room of the house. People used them to dry produce (Josh. 2:6), to sleep on during the hot summer months (1 Sam. 9:25), to wile away the hours in talk, and to pray in private (Acts 10:9).

**Pray that this will not take place in winter (13:18).** Winter is the time of heavy rains in Palestine, flooding roads and wadis.[303] Gadarene refugees during the first revolt sought shelter in Jericho but could not cross the swollen Jordan and

were slain by the Romans.[304] Winter travel is also hazardous if people are to traverse mountain passes.

**Because those will be days of distress unequaled from the beginning (13:19).** All wars bring in their wake horrible suffering. Josephus narrates a lurid tale of terrible famine and a prominent woman cannibalizing her son during the last stages of the siege of Jerusalem as an "act unparalleled in the history whether of Greeks or barbarians and as horrible to relate as it is incredible to hear."[305] Sensationalized stories of cannibalism are not an uncommon feature of siege stories, and this account probably has no factual basis. Josephus simply wanted to convey the horrifying distress that was real.

His description of the terrible inferno that engulfed the city can be verified archaeologically. The Roman soldiers set fire to the temple and the city and plundered and slaughtered the remain-

▶

**MEMORIAL OF THE 10TH ROMAN LEGION**

The pillar commemorates *Legio X Fretensis,* a key army involved in the attack on Jerusalem and the destruction of the temple.

## REFLECTIONS

**JESUS CALLS HIS DISCIPLES TO** place their trust only in him and his words and to abandon their cherished heritage and false trust in the protection of what is now a spiritually bankrupt temple. God will not save it from destruction. Flight is better than fighting for a lost and unworthy cause. Sadly, Israel fought three wars in A.D. 66 – 70 (74), 115 – 17, and 132 – 35, spurred by nationalistic hopes centered on the temple, until the Romans finally expelled them from Jerusalem and made it an entirely forbidden city to Jews. Christians today should be wary of tethering their hopes to nationalistic aspirations or crusades.

◀ *left*

**REMAINS OF THE ROMAN DESTRUCTION OF JERUSALEM**

The skeletal remains of a woman's severed arm found in the charred ruins of a first-century Jewish home in Jerusalem.

ing inhabitants so that "the ground was nowhere visible through the corpses; but the soldiers had to clamber over heaps of bodies in pursuit of the fugitives."[306] The basement of a house in the upper city of Jerusalem was excavated in 1970 and designated the "burnt house" because of the massive amount of ash and soot. Since the coins discovered in the ruins included those minted by the rebels in A.D. 67, 68, and 69 and none is after 70, the conflagration that destroyed this house was caused when the Romans burned the Upper City.[307] Josephus vividly recounts the events (see comments on 13:2).[308]

**Now learn this lesson from the fig tree: As soon as its twigs get tender and its leaves come out, you know that summer is near (13:28).** The fig tree was one of the few deciduous trees in Palestine. Its leafing out is a harbinger of summer. In Isaiah 28:4, the first ripe fig of summer is an image for Israel's defenselessness, and the basket of summer fruit in Amos 8:1 – 2 is an image of judgment.

**I tell you the truth, this generation will certainly not pass away until all these things have happened (13:30).** Josephus laments the fate of Jerusalem at the end of the war. He writes that it was "a city undeserving of these great misfortunes" except that "she produced a generation such as that which caused her overthrow."[309]

**Heaven and earth will pass away, but my words will never pass away (13:31).** This saying affirms the validity of Jesus' prophecy, but the passing away of heaven and earth may not refer to the crumbling of the material universe. It may refer allusively to the temple, which was understood not only as the meeting point of heaven and earth but a miniature replica of heaven and earth.[310] This idea is found in Psalm 78:69, which pictures God as building the sanctuary like the high heavens and the earth. If this reading is correct, it reinforces Jesus' prediction of the temple's destruction (13:2).

**It's like a man going away: He leaves his house and puts his servants in charge, each with his assigned task, and tells the one at the door to keep watch (13:34).** This last parable in Mark picks up on the phrase "right at the door" (13:29). Literally, it reads that the master "gives authority to his slaves, to each one his work." This phrasing matches a papyrus

## REFLECTIONS

**THE KEY ELEMENT IN THE PARABLE IS THAT THE SERVANTS** have no prior warning when the master of the house will return. They must be vigilant, which means "patient waiting at one's post, not speculation about how much longer the delay will be."[A-40] Unceasing vigilance means that Christians will not fall apart when earthly disasters strike, nor will they become spiritually lethargic when others are heralding "peace and safety" (1 Thess. 5:3).

fragment in which a master writes to a slave: "Since for some time you have been my slave-girl, I give you authority henceforth to go wherever you wish without being accused by me."[311]

## The Anointing and Plans for Betrayal (14:1 – 11)

**Now the Passover and the Feast of Unleavened Bread were only two days away (14:1).** In the time of Jesus, the Festival of the Passover Offering, commemorating God's redemption of Israel, had become a national holy day celebrated in Jerusalem. The Passover lambs (one-year-old sheep) were slaughtered on the afternoon of Nisan 14 and eaten in a family or fraternal gathering between sunset and midnight, technically the next day, Nisan 15, since the Jewish day was reckoned from sunset to sunset (cf. Gen. 1:5). The Feast of Unleavened Bread is the seven-day feast following Passover, beginning on Nisan 15.[312] By avoiding bread with yeast and rejoicing in a feast, those unable to journey to Jerusalem or too poor to purchase a sacrificial lamb for Passover could celebrate the festival of Unleavened Bread. The two festivals had essentially become one in the minds of many.[313] Leaven was removed in a ceremonial search of the dwelling on the morning the Passover lambs were sacrificed, and some thought of it as the first day of Unleavened Bread, although technically it began the next day.

**The chief priests and the teachers of the law (14:1).** The "chief priests" in view here were those permanently employed at the temple as an executive committee, overseeing its daily operations. They include the high priest, the captain of the temple (responsible for the worship), and the temple treasurers. Their wealth and power alienated them from the ordinary priests. "The teachers of the law" (scribes) are those scholars allied with the priestly hierarchy.

**"But not during the Feast," they said, "or the people may riot"(14:2).** The fears of the Jewish leaders about a tumult of the people were realistic since Passover was the celebration of the liberation from Egypt, and many viewed it as the prototype of God's final liberation of Israel. It is estimated that anywhere from 85,000 to 300,000 pilgrims converged on Jerusalem, that normally had a population of 25,000 to 30,000, filling it with the sounds and smells of hordes of people and animals. Most pilgrims slept in tents or boarded in the towns of the surrounding countryside.

The chief priests' guards had the main responsibility for policing the city, and the Romans had only a small garrison in Jerusalem. Since the atmosphere in Jerusalem was so explosive at this time of year, the Roman governor moved with more troops from his headquarters in Caesarea to Jerusalem to thwart any violent uprisings. In spite of these precautions, Josephus records numerous protests and riots during the Passover season.

## The Anointing (14:3 – 9)

**A woman came with an alabaster jar of very expensive perfume, made of pure nard. She broke the jar and poured the perfume on his head (14:3).** Jerusalem was filled with a strong smell from the temple sacrifices. If the wind blew from the east, the smoke from the altar turned back not only into the temple courts but over the whole city, bringing a mixture of the horrible reek of burning flesh and the heady smell of incense. Women who could afford it tended to use a great deal

of scent, though the rabbis argued in vain that the incense of the temple ought to be enough for a person.³¹⁴

Anointing was common at feasts (see Luke 7:46: "You did not put oil on my head").³¹⁵ Alabaster jars were made from translucent calcite stone and stood five to nine inches high. A narrow neck restricted the flow of oil or perfume. Breaking the whole jar indicates that its entire contents were used. Nard was a highly valued plant from India. Its value is pegged here at three hundred denarii, which represented almost a year's wage for a day laborer. According to Mark 6:37, two hundred denarii was sufficient to provide a meal for five thousand people.

A social divide existed between male space and female space in the ancient world. Men and women did not intermingle even in the home. Women only crossed into the public male world to wait on men and then retreated.

## The Last Supper (14:12 – 31)

**Judas Iscariot (14:10).** See comments on 3:19.

**On the first day of the Feast of Unleavened Bread, when it was customary to sacrifice the Passover lamb (14:12).**

On the eve of Passover, work normally ceased at noon. The ritual slaughter of the Passover lambs began around 3:00 P.M. as the heads of the household brought their animals to the temple.³¹⁶ The priests sprinkled the blood of the lamb against the base of the altar and offered the fat on the altar. With the legs unbroken and the head still attached to the carcass, it was wrapped in its skin and returned to the worshipers. The forecourt of the temple had been the place to eat the meal, but the large number of people made that now impossible. It was only stipulated that the meal had to be eaten in Jerusalem with a minimum of ten persons. This took place in the evening on Nisan 15 — strictly speaking, the first day of Unleavened Bread.

**A man carrying a jar of water will meet you (14:13).** Since Jesus probably stays with Simon the Leper in Bethany, his company probably enters Jerusalem either through the Fountain Gate by the

◀ *left*

**PERFUME JARS**

Ointment jars and surgical instruments dating to the Hellenistic era.

◀

**PASSOVER TEMPLE SCENE**

A model of the sacrificial altar in the court of priests of the Jerusalem temple.

Gihon Spring, the Casemate Gate or Water Gate by the King's Garden, or the Potsherd Gate near the pool of Siloam. It would be usual to spot someone carrying a water jar at any of these gates,[317] but it would be unusual to find a man doing so, since women normally fetched water.

**He will show you a large upper room, furnished and ready (14:15).** The upper room was "a smaller box on top of a bigger box."[318] It was used as a guest room, storeroom, and a place of retreat; such a room was usually reached by an outside stairway that allowed one to enter it without going through the main room of the house. The sages met their students in upper rooms to teach, according to later rabbinic traditions. This room apparently was furnished with a table that would have been a low U-shaped one. Couches or cushions would have been used for reclining at the meal.

**One who dips bread into the bowl with me (14:20).** Diners shared from the same dish and used the bread as their utensil. In this culture, eating bread with someone barred one from hostile acts against a fellow eater (see Ps. 41:9). In *The Sen-*

*right* ▶

**BETHANY**

The site of the ancient village of Bethany.

**THE UPPER ROOM**

A historical tradition locates the last supper in the Cenacle on Mount Zion. This present structure was reconstructed by Franciscans in 1335.

*tences of the Syriac Menander* 2.215 – 16 we find this admonition: "And he with whom you had a meal, do not walk with him in a treacherous way."

**While they were eating, Jesus took bread, gave thanks and broke it, and gave it to his disciples, saying, "Take it; this is my body" (14:22).** The visible union between Jesus and his disciples will dissolve at his death, but he provides a symbol by which it is to be replaced by an invisible one. He gives a special interpretation of the shared loaf and the shared wine, linked to the familiar rite of pronouncing a blessing before a meal. At every meal, the head of the family took the bread, lifted it up, and said, "Praise be Thou, O Lord our God, King of the Universe, who causes bread to come forth from the earth." After the "Amen" response, the bread was broken and distributed, mediating the blessing to each one who ate. Jesus gives the traditional blessing of the bread a new twist by saying that it is his body.

**Then he took the cup (14:23).** The *Book of Jubilees* provides evidence for the association of wine with the Passover festival (*Jub.* 49:6). Wine was always diluted with at least three parts water to one part wine (2 Macc. 15:39).

**They all drank from it (14:23).** Jesus uses the suggestive symbolism of the wine as the blood of the grape, plucked from the vine and crushed. Drinking the cup of someone was understood as a means of entering into a communion relationship with that person to the point that one shared that person's destiny, for good or ill (see Ps. 16:4 – 5).

**I tell you the truth, I will not drink again of the fruit of the vine until that day when I drink it anew in the kingdom of God (14:25).** "Not drinking again" becomes a metaphor for death.[319] With this statement, Jesus again prophesies his death. He will die before he will join in another festive banquet.[320] "Drinking again" is a metaphor for God's saving action when his kingdom comes.

**When they had sung a hymn, they went out to the Mount of Olives (14:26).** We should not immediately associate this hymn with the Hallel Psalms sung at Passover. The Passover rituals known to us from the Mishnah developed after the destruction of the temple when it no longer was a pilgrimage feast. Before then, the Passover practices were not uniform; and these later traditions may not have been the custom in Jesus' day. The hymn may simply convey the "prayerful context as the meal closed."[321]

**Tonight — before the rooster crows twice (14:30).** The cock's crow may refer to a real rooster crowing or to the bugle call of the *gallicinium* (cockcrow) that signaled the third watch of the night in Roman military reckoning (from 12:00 to 3:00 A.M.). The two cockcrows may refer to the signals at the beginning and the end of that watch. The text, however, lacks the definite article before the word for rooster, and this absence suggests that Mark understands it to refer to a fowl rather than a night watch.

Rabbinic evidence conflicts on whether one was allowed to raise poultry in the city of Jerusalem. A tradition from the Mishnah forbids it;[322] a tradition from the Jerusalem Talmud assumes their presence in the city.[323] Whether or not this conflicting testimony is relevant for the first century, a rooster would not need to have been within the walls of Jerusalem to have been heard.

The second cockcrow was connected to the dawn or rising sun.[324] Jesus' statement essentially means "before the next dawn."[325]

## Prayer in Gethsemane (14:32 – 52)

**They went to a place called Gethsemane (14:32).** The word Gethsemane comes from a Hebrew/Aramaic word (*Gatz šᵉmānî*), meaning "oil press." Mark does not identify it as a garden (John 18:1)

| Contrasts Between Passover and the Lord's Supper | |
|---|---|
| Passover | Lord's Supper |
| In the old age of law | In the new age of the kingdom |
| The great festival meal celebrating the birth of God's people | The new celebratory meal of the birth of God's people |
| Participants associate themselves with deliverance and the old covenant | Participants associate themselves with redemption and the new covenant |
| Looks back to the Exodus and forward to God's salvation | Looks back to the cross and forward to the consummation |

but simply as a "place"; four different locations on the Mount of Olives claim the honor of being the authentic site. Taylor contends that Gethsemane does not refer to an olive grove but to a spacious cave (about 55 feet long and 29-1/2 feet wide) within a cultivated enclosure, adjacent to the Church of All Nations, where olives were pressed for oil.[326] The press would have been in operation in the fall and winter after the olive harvest but would have been idle and used only for storage in the spring. Such a locale, close to the city, would have made an excellent place to spend a chilly night that had others kindling fires for warmth (14:54). It would have been "warm, dry, and roomy, with a cistern inside for water."[327] This location may explain why the young man there is attired only in a linen garment (14:51 – 52) as he presumably sleeps on his cloak. In the shelter of the cave, such a decision is understandable; out in the open, exposed to frigid air, it is not. Jesus may have left the cave to go further away in the enclosure to pray by himself.

Taylor cites as the earliest evidence for its location Egeria's account of her pilgrimage to the Holy Land. She said that pilgrims go "into Gethsemane" and are given candles "so that all can see." Theodosius, in the sixth century, explicitly identifies it as a cave. [328]

**He fell to the ground and prayed that if possible the hour might pass from him (14:35).** The normal Jewish attitude of prayer was to lift one's hands toward heaven and to pray aloud while standing. When one was in particular distress, one prayed lying prostrate. Jesus prostrates himself before his Father to pray in the same way that others in Mark's story fell before him to make their requests (5:22; 7:25).

Jewish prayers are sometimes remarkable for their loud complaint and directness. They approach God as a trusting child does, willing to complain bitterly and ask for anything. These prayers may seem insolent to us, but they reveal an intimacy with God, who is believed to listen sympathetically and grant requests.[329] Jesus' prayer conforms to this tradition. He trusts completely in God as his Father and is obedient.

**Abba, Father (14:36).** "Abba" is the Aramaic word term for father, and there is "no evidence in the literature of pre-Christian or first-century Palestinian Judaism that 'abbā' was used in any sense as a personal address for God by an individual."[330] This unusual way of addressing God was remembered by Jesus' followers because his disciples also experienced such closeness to God in prayer through the Spirit (Rom. 8:15; Gal. 4:6). The term does not mean, "Daddy," however.[331] In translating it for Greek readers, Mark uses the regular word for "father" (*patēr*), not a diminutive form. The word was used both by children for their father and by disciples for an esteemed teacher. While the address

## REFLECTIONS

**JESUS LEARNS GOD'S WILL IN THE** face of evil in exactly the same way we do—through prayer. Jesus overcomes intense distress with intense prayer. Mark teaches us how to pray from Jesus' example. He describes his bearing, his intimate address, his confession of God's omnipotence, his plea to be spared suffering, and his obedient submission to God's will. His posture conveys his helplessness apart from God's enablement and his submission to God's will. He prays desiring God's deliverance but accepting the cup of suffering. Having prostrated himself before God, Jesus can now stand before men.

may exhibit intimacy, it is not flippant. As Father, God requires obedience.

**Now the betrayer had arranged a signal with them: "The one I kiss is the man" (14:44).** One normally greeted a teacher or rabbi with a kiss on the hand or cheek if one considered oneself to be an equal (see Luke 7:45, "You did not give me a kiss"). See the parting kiss given to Paul by the Ephesian elders (Acts 20:37). Judas addresses him as rabbi and kisses him (Mark 14:45). He may have kissed him affectionately (the same word appears in Luke 15:20) or on the hand or even the foot (Luke 7:38, 45). The customary greeting of respect is turned into a sign of infamy and death.

**Am I leading a rebellion . . . that you have come out with swords and clubs to capture me? (14:48).** The high priests paid Judas to lead them to Jesus where they can quietly arrest him without a skirmish, yet they come ready for combat.

The question, "Am I leading a rebellion?" interprets the Greek phrase, "Have you come out against a robber?" Josephus uses the term "robber" for the social bandits that badgered the aristocracy. He "never uses the term *lēstēs* to describe a revolutionary against Rome."[332] These bandits were usually peasants driven from their land. In response to injustice, they chose outlawry rather than meek submission and preyed on the rich in the countryside. Galilee was famous as a haven for bandits; Josephus notes their "habitual malpractices, theft, robbery, and rapine."[333]

Yet Mark is writing in a time during or shortly after the Jewish revolt against Rome. He may intend for readers to see the clear contrast between Jesus and contemporary assassins and revolutionaries.

**A young man, wearing nothing but a linen garment, was following Jesus (14:51).** This man apparently was sleeping in his undergarment, a linen cloth, and attempts to follow along with Jesus. When the arresting posse tries to seize him, he wriggles free from their grasp, fleeing into the darkness naked (presumably with only his loin cloth).

The young man is unidentified. Some, appealing to John 18:15, identify him as "[the other] disciple" known to the high priest, perhaps John, son of Zebedee. Others have guessed it is Mark himself, whose mother Mary has a house in Jerusalem (Acts 12:12). Remembering his disgrace, Mark gives himself a cameo role in his Gospel. It is more likely, however, that this anonymous figure epitomizes the "save yourself if you can" mentality that causes all the disciples to desert Jesus in a panic. Unprepared for testing, they break down completely, just as Jesus prophesied they would (Mark 14:27). The last remnant of their respectability is stripped away.

## The Sanhedrin Hearing (14:53 – 65)

**They took Jesus to the high priest (14:53).** We learn from Acts 4:6 that the high priest was Joseph Caiaphas, the son-in-law of Annas (who held the office from A.D. 6 until he was deposed in A.D.15). Annas remained a kind of godfather controlling the reins of power with five sons holding the office of high priest.[334] The clan of Annas is remembered in the Babylonian Talmud for its knavery: "Woe unto me because of the house of Hanin [Annas], woe unto me because of their whisperings."[335] Josephus refers to the son of Annas, Ananas II (high priest in A.D. 62), as following the school of the Sadducees, who were "more heartless than any of the other Jews . . . when they sit in judgment."[336]

Pilate's predecessor, Valerius Gratus, removed four high priests during his eleven-year tenure as governor. Caiaphas had to be an artful politician to have held office as high priest for eighteen years from A.D. 18 to 36, serving throughout Pilate's tenure.[337] The family tomb of Caiaphas has been discovered. The name of Joseph bar Caiaphas is inscribed in Aramaic (*Yhwsp br Qp'*) on an elaborately decorated bone box containing the bones of a sixty-year-old man.[338]

We do not know where the high priest's home was. Some suggest it was located on the old Hasmonean palace on the West Hill of Jerusalem that "stood above the Xystus on the opposite side of the upper town."[339] Others claim it was near the Zion Gate in the southern section of the Western Hill.

**The chief priests, elders and teachers of the law came together (14:53).** In addition to the chief priests (see comments on 14:1), this group may also include the leader of the weekly course of priests and the leaders of the daily courses of priests. The elders are likely the heads of the distinguished families who are not priests but are aligned with the governing priestly faction. They are distinct from the elders who were the scholars behind "the tradition of the elders" (7:5).

**The chief priests and the whole Sanhedrin (14:55).** The Mishnah identifies the Great Sanhedrin as consisting of seventy-one members (see Num. 11:16).[340] The Mishnah, however, is not a reliable source for understanding how this body functioned in the first century or the juridical procedure against Jesus. The term *sanhedrin* can denote any council (see Mark 13:9, "councils," lit., "sanhedrins"). Rather than referring to a fixed body of members suddenly called into session in the middle of the night, it is more likely an ad hoc group of powerful noblemen, a sanhedrin of judges, whom the high priest assembles for an inquest to prepare charges before Pilate.

The Jewish people did not have the right to administer capital punishment at this time (John 18:31). The Jerusalem Talmud states: "Forty years before the destruction of the Temple, the right to judge capital cases was withdrawn."[341] It was the most jealously guarded of all the attributes of government. According to Josephus, the high priest Ananus was deposed for convening a Sanhedrin that condemned James, the brother of Jesus, to death during a transition from one governor to the next; he was accused of acting without the governor's permission.[342] The Sanhedrin gathered to judge Jesus, therefore, cannot pronounce a real death sentence because only Pilate, the governor, can carry out the death penalty after reaching his own verdict. He is not

# ▶ The So-Called Illegalities of Jesus' Trial

The trial described by Mark is highly irregular according to rules listed in the Mishnah tractate *Sanhedrin* concerning the procedure for courts conducting capital trials.

(1) Capital cases were to be tried during the daytime, and the verdict must be reached during the daytime (*m. Sanh.* 4:1).

(2) Trials were not to be conducted on a Sabbath eve or on the eve of a festival day (*m. Sanh.* 4:1; see Acts 12:4, which reports that Herod intended to bring Peter to the people *after the Passover*).

(3) Capital cases were supposed to begin with reasons for acquittal and not with reasons for conviction (*m. Sanh.* 4:1). Attempts were to be made to find witnesses and arguments for the defense. If on the way to stoning someone should say, "I have somewhat to argue in favor of his acquittal," or even if the accused does so, they bring him back four or five times. The herald was to cry: "Such a one, the son of such a one is going to be stoned for he committed such or such an offense. Such and such are witnesses against him. If any man knoweth aught in favor of his acquittal let him come and plead it" (*m. Sanh.* 5:4). A later rabbinic tradition imagines that this was indeed done in Jesus' case:

On the Eve of Passover Yeshu [one text adds the Nazarean] was hanged. Forty days before his execution took place, a herald went forth and cried, "He is going forth to be stoned because he practised sorcery and enticed Israel to apostasy. Any one who can say anything in his favour, let him come forward and plead on his behalf." But since nothing was brought forward in his favour he was hanged on the eve of Passover![A-41]

(4) Verdicts of acquittal could be reached on the same day, but verdicts of conviction must be confirmed on the following day after a night's sleep (*m. Sanh.* 4:1).

(5) Condemnation required the evidence of two witnesses.[A-42] When witnesses disagreed, their evidence was null and void (*m. Sanh.* 5:2). If they were found to be false witnesses, they were required to suffer the "same death-penalty to which the accused had been made liable."[A-43]

(6) The Mishnah assumes that the Sanhedrin met in the inner courts of temple, the Chamber of Hewn Stone, not in the high priest's home.[A-44]

Mark's report of Jesus' trial depicts the nation's religious leaders gathering furtively in the middle of the night and conducting a hasty and blatantly prejudicial proceeding against Jesus. Some scholars have concluded that Mark has invented the Jewish hearing to transfer Roman guilt for Jesus' arrest and crucifixion to the Jews. But this Mishnaic tractate, compiled around A.D. 220, reflects the circumstances and scruples of a later era. The laws regarding capital cases in Mishnah *Sanhedrin* may not be representative of the historical procedure for the Sanhedrin in the first century or, for that matter, any period. They are idealized and theoretical, assuming, for example, that the king rules, not a high priest under the thumb of a Roman governor. The laws for the Sanhedrin are perceived through the lens of the wishful thinking of the post-war rabbis who compiled the oral law — this is the way it should be when the temple is restored, and it is assumed that this is the way it must have always been.

A Sanhedrin controlled by the high priest was also unlikely to follow Pharisaic procedures. If it were an informal hearing gathering evidence to bring to the governor, it would not need to observe legal formalities. According to Deuteronomy 18:20, a false prophet is to be killed immediately — even on a feast day. The chief priests considered Jesus such a serious threat that they made every effort to eliminate him by getting the Roman governor to put him to death and discredit him forever with death by crucifixion.

a rubber stamp and can overrule whatever they decide.

**I will destroy this man-made temple and in three days will build another, not made by man. (14:58).** Mark describes this as false testimony, and it is difficult to identify precisely how it is false. Possibly, the Jewish leaders wish to paint Jesus as a dangerous crank. Josephus describes the false Egyptian prophet gathering followers on the Mount of Olives and promising that at his command the walls of Jerusalem will fall down.[343] They may want to associate this boast with Jesus' claim to be the Messiah. Since 2 Samuel 7:13 mentions that David's offspring will build a house for God's name, some may have assumed that one of the tasks of the coming Messiah was to rebuild the temple (see Zech. 6:12 – 13). The Targum to Isaiah 53:5 reads: "But he shall build the sanctuary that was polluted because of our transgressions and given up because of our iniquities. . . ."[344]

"Without human hands" (NIV "not made by man"; cf. Dan. 2:34, 45) means not of human origin. It will be a spiritual sanctuary.[345]

**The high priest tore his clothes (14:63).** Tearing one's garments was an ancient way of expressing distress and mourning.[346] The gesture is a fitting response to blasphemy and a dramatic way of getting the others to agree with him.

**You have heard the blasphemy (14:64).** According to Mishnah *Sanhedrin* 7:5, " 'The blasphemer' is not culpable unless he pronounces the Name itself" (see Lev. 24:16). Measured by this rule, Jesus is not technically guilty. This ruling may not have been operative in Jesus' time, and what people regard as sacrilege need not fit any technical definition. Jesus' admission that he is the Messiah supposedly infringes on God's prerogative to declare who the Messiah is and to enthrone him.

Jesus' answer that the Son of Man will be sitting at the right hand of God in power also implies that he is on the same level with God. The Talmud records a dispute in which Rabbi Akiba interprets the phrase in Daniel 7:9, "till thrones were placed," as referring to two thrones, one for God and one for David (the Messiah), so that "one like a son of man is identified as the royal Messiah." His colleagues vigorously reject this interpretation as profaning the Divine Presence.[347]

A text from Qumran refers to the last enemy of God calling himself the son of the Most High and demanding adoration and obedience.[348] Flusser calls it "important evidence for a Jewish tradition about the superhuman hubris of the Antichrist."[349] Jesus' assertion perhaps

▶

**HIGH PRIEST**

Artistic interpretation of the Jewish high priest.

confirms the high priest's suspicions that Jesus is a figure like this who tries to seduce the world.

In his summary of the Jewish law, Josephus freely renders Leviticus 24:16: "Let him that blasphemeth God be stoned, then hung for a day, and buried ignominiously and in obscurity."[350] The high priest may not be able to stone Jesus, but he has every intention that Jesus be put to death and suffer the humiliation of being hanged and given a dishonorable burial.

**Then some began to spit at him; they blindfolded him, struck him with their fists, and said, "Prophesy!" (14:65).** The taunt to prophesy derives from Jesus' implicit claim to be the Messiah, who was supposed to have a prophetic gift. According to an anecdote in the Babylonian Talmud, the Messiah is able to judge by smell:

Bar Koziba ["son of lies," see comments on 13:6] reigned two and a half years, then said to the rabbis, "I am the messiah." They answered, "Of the messiah it is written that he smells and judges; let us see whether he can do so." When they saw that he was unable to judge by scent, they slew him.[351]

**REFLECTIONS**

**THESE EVENTS REVEAL THAT GOD'S** power is revealed in weakness, and they confirm that Jesus indeed is the Messiah and the Son of God. Humans have always stumbled over how one whom they assume should be associated with power and glory could possibly be linked to suffering and death. The mystery of God's love and power expressed in the cross consequently remains a riddle to many.

The torturers may also be playing a cruel version of the game of blindman's bluff, known from this era, where the person must guess who is hitting him.[352]

## Peter's Denial (14:66 – 72)

**While Peter was below in the courtyard (14:66).** Peter's denial of Jesus wraps around the trial of Jesus, indicating that they both take place at the same time. While Jesus is interrogated by the high priest, Peter waits in the courtyard (though the word *aulē* may refer to a court in the house). The courtyard was the open space around which rooms were arranged; the "entryway" (14:68) was the vestibule leading to the courtyard.

**Surely you are one of them, for you are a Galilean (14:70).** In rabbinic literature, Galileans are portrayed as simpletons and riffraff (see the prejudice reflected in John 7:45 – 52). They can be identified by their Aramaic accents (Matt. 26:73). Jerusalem merchants taunt a Galilean wanting to purchase an *amar*:

"Foolish Galilean," they said to him, "do you mean an 'ass' for riding [*hamār*], 'wine' to drink [*hamar*], 'wool' for clothing [*'amar*] or a 'lamb' for killing [*immar*]?"[353]

Vermes explains with an example from modern British English: "In careless everyday conversation the Galileans dropped their aitches."[354]

**He began to call down curses on himself (14:71).** The text does not say that Peter called down curses on himself. The verb has no object in the Greek text, and it is possible to construe it that he goes so far as to curse Jesus. Pliny the Younger was appointed by the emperor Trajan to govern Bithynia-Pontus and reported that he asked suspected Christians three times with threats of punishment, "Are you a Christian?"[355] The accused proved their innocence by cursing Jesus, which, he says, "those who are really Christians cannot be made to do."[356] In the *Martyrdom of Polycarp* 9:3, the proconsul adjures Polycarp, "Swear and I will release you." Polycarp replies, "How can I blaspheme the King who saved me?"

### The Trial Before Pilate (15:1 – 20)

**Very early in the morning (15:1).** The working day of a Roman official began at the earliest hour of daylight. Seneca attests that Roman trials could begin at daybreak.[357] Pliny completed his work by 10:00 A.M.; Vespasian finished before dawn.[358] If the council spent the early hours of daylight examining Jesus, they may have been too late for Pilate's tribunal.

**They bound Jesus, led him away and handed him over to Pilate (15:1).** Pilate's

COINS MINTED UNDER PONTIUS PILATE

official title was prefect (see inscription found in Caesarea identifying him as *Praefectus Iudaeae*). The governors were called procurators only after A.D. 44. As governor, Pilate had the power of life and death over all the inhabitants of his province.[359] He was of equestrian rank (knight, wealthy enough to own a horse). In this rank, he would have had no assistants of a similar status and no team of Roman officials to handle all of the administrative matters. A large part of the everyday chores of government and administration was thus carried out by the local councils and magistrates. They had the power to arrest, take evidence, and make a preliminary examination in order to present a case before a governor for a formal trial. The Roman authorities held them accountable for outbreaks of violence and would replace them. The governor, however, was ultimately responsible for ensuring that order was maintained and for deciding the death penalty.

**The chief priests accused him of many things (15:3).** No criminal code existed for the non-Roman citizen tried in the provinces. It was technically known as a "trial outside the system." The governor was free to make his own rules and judgments as he saw fit, to accept or reject charges, and within reason to fashion whatever penalties he chose. Governors,

---

### ▶ Pilate

Pilate was nominated to his post in A.D. 26 by Lucius Aelius Sejanus as the fifth Roman prefect of Judea. Sejanus rose to become the prefect of the Praetorian Guard under Tiberius and became his trusted advisor. He gained greater influence in the affairs of government when the moody Tiberius retired to Campania and Capri in 27 and handled most of the government affairs and complaints.[A-45] In 31, he was named

consul with Tiberius, which made him de facto joint emperor and the heir apparent. According to Philo, Sejanus manifested anti-Semitic attitudes and attacked the Jewish inhabitants of Rome with slander because he wished to do away with the nation.[A-46] Under the sponsorship of the powerful Sejanus in Rome, Pilate did not fear repercussions from his various run-ins with the Jewish sensibilities in Palestine.

*continued next page*

*continued*

We get the impression from Josephus that Pilate believed staunchly in Roman sovereignty and wished to ram it down the Judeans' throat. When he first arrived, he brought in army standards with Roman religious symbols into Jerusalem under the cover of night and precipitated a riotous reaction. Crowds thronged to Caesarea, where they bared their necks to the Roman swords, forcing him to back down.[A-47] Later, he confiscated funds from the treasury to finance an aqueduct from Bethlehem to Jerusalem. Another disturbance followed with many killed.[A-48] At some point, he was responsible for the deaths of Galileans whose blood was mingled with their sacrifices (Luke 13:1–2). His last outrage occurred when he heard that a prophet in Samaria had gathered with a crowd to uncover sacred vessels buried by Moses. Pilate overreacted with a preemptive strike and wiped them out. The Samaritans protested, and Pilate was recalled to Rome in 36.[A-49]

On October 18, 31, Sejanus conspired to grab power completely for himself. The plot was uncovered, and Tiberius had him executed hours later. What was known as the Tiberian terror followed, uprooting all of Sejanus's supporters. No one who had been associated with Sejanus and his policies could feel secure. Philo contended that a dramatic change in policy toward the Jews also occurred:

> Tiberius... knew at once after Sejanus's death that the accusations made against the inhabitants of Rome were false slanders.... And he charged his procurators on every place to which they were appointed to speak comfortably to the members of our nation in the different cities assuring them that the penal measures did not extend to all but only to the guilty, who were few, and to disturb none of the established customs but even to regard them as a trust committed to their care, the people as naturally peaceable, and the institutions as an influence promoting orderly conduct.[A-50]

Philo regarded Pilate as an agent of Sejanus's policy, and this information may help make sense of Pilate's behavior as it is reported in the Gospels. He describes Pilate as "naturally inflexible, a blend of self-will and relentlessness," stubborn, vindictive, hot tempered, but afraid that the Jews would report to the emperor "his briberies, insults, robberies, outrages and wanton injuries."[A-51] After the Sejanian conspiracy was exposed, Pilate was vulnerable. He could not chance a Jewish appeal to Rome and had to demonstrate unwavering loyalty to Tiberius.

Pilate served a long time in his office, and Josephus gives an anecdote explaining Tiberius's policy of appointing governors:

> Once a man lay wounded, and a swarm of flies hovered about his wounds. A passer-by took pity on his evil plight and, in the belief that he did not raise a hand because he could not, was about to step up and shoo them off. The wounded man, however, begged him to think no more of doing anything about it. At this the man spoke up and asked him why he was not interested in escaping from his wretched condition, "Why," said he, "you would put me in a worse condition if you drove them off? For since these flies have already had their fill of blood, they no longer feel such pressing need to annoy me but are in some measure slack. But if others were to come with fresh appetite, they would take over my now weakened body and that would indeed be the death of me." He too, he said, for the same reason took the precaution of not dispatching governors continually to the subject peoples who had been brought to ruin by so many thieves; for the governors would harry them utterly like flies. Their natural appetite for plunder would be reinforced by their expectation of being speedily deprived of that pleasure. The record of Tiberius's acts will bear out my account of his humor in such matters. For during the twenty-two years that he was emperor he sent altogether two men, Gratus and Pilate, his successor, to govern the Jewish nation.[A-52]

however, tended to follow the legal custom with which they were familiar.

Trials normally took place in a public setting before the governor, who sat on his tribunal. Since there were no public prosecutors, a prosecution's case was brought by private third parties, who presented formal charges (cf. the trials of Paul, Acts 24:1 – 9; 25:1 – 27).

The Roman governor would not have put anyone on trial for his life simply for transgressing Jewish religious regulations. When Paul was arrested, the Roman garrison commander wrote to the governor Felix in Caesarea, "I found that the accusation had to do with questions about their law, but there was no charge against him that deserved death or imprisonment" (Acts 23:29; see the reaction of Gallio in 18:14 – 17). The Sanhedrin may have found Jesus guilty of blasphemy and deserving of death, but a religious charge would not suffice for Pilate to take action. The governor only cared that matters religious did not become matters political. The chief priests must thus formulate a charge that will capture his attention and carry a death sentence. The charges need to be political, which explains why Pilate asks Jesus, "Are you the king of the Jews?" (Mark 15:2). Charges of *maiestas*, "the diminution of the majesty of the Roman people," were increasingly frequent under Tiberius.[360]

Josephus bemoaned the various would-be kings who rose up and caused disturbances:

> And so Judaea was filled with brigandage. Anyone might make himself king as the head of a band of rebels whom he fell in with, and then would press on to the destruction of the community, causing trouble to few Romans and then only to a small degree but bringing the greatest slaughter upon their own people.[361]

**Now it was the custom at the Feast to release a prisoner whom the people requested (15:6).** This tradition may derive from the days of the Hasmonean kings, and the Romans may have continued it when it suited their purposes. A papyrus from A.D. 85 contains a report of judicial proceedings before the prefect of Egypt and quotes the words from the governor to the prisoner: "You were worthy of scourging . . . but I will give you to the people."[362] A text from the Mishnah rules, "They may slaughter (the Passover lamb) . . . for one whom they (the authorities) have promised to release from prison."[363]

**A man called Barabbas (15:7).** The name Barabbas means "son of Abba." This name distinguishes him from others with the same personal name.

**The crowd came up and asked Pilate to do for them what he usually did (15:8).** Governors were known to enter into conversation with the crowd, although a first-century papyrus warns against this since it may lead to injustice. The crowd is probably composed of partisans supporting the priestly hierarchy. It would be easy to stir them up if they were led to believe that Jesus has somehow threatened the temple. The temple was not only a potent religious symbol, it provided employment to a large segment of the population of Jerusalem.

## The Mocking and Crucifixion of Jesus (15:15 – 41)

**He had Jesus flogged, and handed him over to be crucified (15:15).** Scourging was a customary preliminary to crucifixion. The prisoner was bound to a pillar or post and beaten with a *flagellum*. This whip consisted of leather thongs plaited with pieces of bone, lead, or bronze or with hooks and was appropriately called a scorpion. Gladiators sometimes fought with them. There was no prescribed number of lashes so that in some cases the scourging itself was fatal. The balls would cause deep contusions as the flesh was literally ripped into bloody ribbons. It was so horrible that Suetonius claimed even Domitian was horrified by it.[364] Significant blood loss could also occur, critically weakening the victim.

**The soldiers led Jesus away into the palace (that is, the Praetorium) (15:16).** During his sojourns to Jerusalem, Pilate probably stayed in the luxurious palace of Herod the Great (near the Tower of David and the Jaffa Gate), the highest point in the city. Philo recalls that when Pilate was first appointed governor he stayed in Herod's palace.[365] Others argue that he resided in the Antonia Fortress (named after Mark Anthony) adjacent to the northwest corner of the temple; it served as the barracks for the Roman cohort. It seems more likely that the governor would choose to lodge in Herod's more opulent palace.

**They put a purple robe on him (15:17).** The mocking of Jesus by the soldiers is intended to parody the charge that he is king of the Jews. The purple cloak probably refers to the oblong-shaped garment fastened around the neck by a brooch that was a foot soldier's equipment (*chlamys*), or perhaps the cloak of the lictor. According to Suetonius, Caligula wore one.[366] It is intended to be a mock royal robe.[367]

**They twisted together a crown of thorns and set it on him (15:17).** This crown may or may not be an instrument of torture. The soldiers are improvising and grab whatever is at hand. Thus the thorns may come from a type of palm tree common to Jerusalem, a dwarf date palm or thorn palm, which grew as an ornamental and had formidable spikes. The leaves could be easily woven and the long spikes from the date palm inserted to resemble a radiate crown.[368] Evidence for this type of crown is found in seals excavated from

◀

**TREE USED FOR MAKING CROWN OF THORNS**

◀ *left*

**SOLDIER GAMES**

A Roman era pavement inscribed with lines related to "the king's game."

the Roman camp in Jerusalem. Or, the soldiers may have simply grabbed a clump of thorns and put them on his head like a cap.

**Hail, king of the Jews! (15:18).** The homage of the soldiers parodies that given to the emperor, "Ave Caesar, victor, imperator." Philo records similar mockery of an imbecile named Carabas in Alexandria. He was used as a stand-in to lampoon Herod Agrippa I when he was proclaimed king of Judea.[369]

**A certain man from Cyrene, Simon, the father of Alexander and Rufus (15:21).** The names are Greek and Latin, although Simon may reflect the Hebrew Simeon. If Simon is a Jew, which seems likely, he may have been a member of the synagogue of Cyrenians that later opposed Stephen (Acts 6:9). Apparently, Rufus and Alexander are known to the first readers of this Gospel. A Rufus is mentioned in Romans 16:13 and in Polycarp's letter to the Philippians 9:1. An ossuary with the name "Alexander, son of Simon" has been discovered in Jerusalem.[370]

**They forced him to carry the cross (15:21).** Normally, a condemned person carried the crossbeam (*patibulum*) to the crucifixion site, where a vertical post (*stipes, staticulum*) had already been fixed in the ground. Wood was scarce, and crosses were probably used more than once. Plutarch says that "every criminal who goest to execution must carry his own cross on his back."[371]

Mark does not tell us why Jesus is unable to carry his own cross. We can surmise that he was too weak or too slow after the ordeal of his scourging, which also may explain his quick death (15:44). Cicero mentions an executioner's hook used to drag the condemned to the place of execution.[372] "Compel" is a technical term for commandeering a person or his property (see Matt. 5:41). Simon is grabbed from the crowd and forced to carry the crossbeam to the place where Jesus will be crucified.

**They brought Jesus to the place called Golgotha (which means The Place of the Skull) (15:22).** According to Roman law (and Jewish, Lev. 24:14), crucifixion was to take place outside the city. Quintilian commended crucifixion as a deterrent and noted that the executioners chose "the most crowded roads where the most people can see and be moved by this fear."[373] Josephus reports that during the siege of Jerusalem, the Romans crucified five hundred or more victims every day opposite the wall, nailing their victims in different postures as a spectacle for those in the city.[374] The crucifixion site would be near roads leading into the city

---

# REFLECTIONS

## THE IRONIC RECOGNITION OF JESUS

is now complete. He was "anointed" by a woman in the home of a leper but it was for his burial (14:3 – 9). He was identified as the Christ (the Anointed One), the son of the Blessed One, by the high priest, who declares it blasphemy. He was announced as king by Pilate (15:17 – 19) and saluted by the soldiers (15:16 – 19). These anoint him with spit, crown him with thorns, and will soon enthrone him on a cross.[A-53] One scholar writes: "So powerful is the kingdom that it reaches down even into the hate-filled minds and venomous lips of its foes, drawing unwitting testimony from those who look without seeing."[A-54]

where people could learn what happens to malefactors and would-be kings.

Jesus is taken to a place called Golgotha, which Mark interprets for his Greek-speaking readers as "skull place." The more familiar term Calvary derives from the Latin translation *calvaria*, which means "skull". The name Golgotha does not appear in any other extant source from antiquity other than the Gospels. The name may refer to (1) the shape of the outcropping of rock that resembled a skull, (2) the place where executions were carried out, or (3) a region that included the place of execution and a cultivated tract of land where there were tombs.[375] This last option seems best. Taylor concludes:

Golgotha was probably an oval-shaped abandoned quarry located west of the second wall, north of the first wall. Jesus may have been crucified in the southern part of this area, just outside the Gennath Gate, and near the road going west, but at a site visible also from the road north and buried some 200 m. away to the north, in a quieter part of Golgotha where there were tombs and gardens.[376]

This site is not far from the Gennath (Gardens) Gate mentioned by Josephus; it was located in the first wall and fits John's mention of a garden in the place (John 19:41).[377] Exposed rock in this area shows evidence of ancient quarrying, and it may have been a rejected portion of an ancient preexilic white stone quarry. One scholar suggests that the early Christians knew that Golgotha was a rejected quarry stone, which brings to mind Psalm 118:22, mentioned in Mark 12:10 (see also Acts 4:11 and 1 Peter 2:7).[378]

Constantine drew on local tradition to build "a great sacred enclave" in this area in 325 – 35.[379] The Church of the Holy Sepulchre is currently located on this site. Despite this ancient tradition, several questions remain. Was it outside the city wall in the first century? Was it not too close to the temple (and the palace of Herod)? Since the prevailing winds came from the west, nearly all extant tombs are found to the north, east, and south of Jerusalem. Did the Gennath Gate open onto a roadway?

**Then they offered him wine mixed with myrrh (15:23).** According to a Talmudic tradition, the women of Jerusalem offered a narcotic drink to people condemned to death in order to alleviate the pain of execution, but it refers to wine and frankincense (see Prov. 31:6 – 7).[380] The text, however, implies that the executioners, not pious women, offer the drink. Pliny regarded the finest wine as that "spiced with the scent of myrrh."[381] The Romans did not consider it to be intoxicating but more of a woman's drink.[382] The executioners may have given this drink to exhausted prisoners on the way to the place of execution to give them more strength so that they would last longer and suffer longer.

Another possibility is that this gesture continues the mocking of Jesus as a triumphant king. At the end of a Roman triumphant procession, the triumphator is offered a cup of ceremonial wine that he refuses to drink but pours out on the altar at the moment of sacrifice.[383]

Jesus rejects the offer of wine because he has made a vow of abstinence at the Last Supper (14:25) and wishes to remain fully conscious to the bitter end. He will drink the Father's cup instead (14:36).

**They crucified him (15:24).** Mark does not need to describe crucifixion to his readers since they would be familiar with it. The victim is stripped to increase the humiliation and fastened to the crossbeam with nails and/or ropes. The executioners lift up the crossbeam with forked poles until the victim's feet clear the ground and then attach it to the stake. Most guess that "Jesus' cross stood some 7 ft. high."[384] Since the nails do not support the whole body, a plank (*sedile, sedecula*) is fastened to the *stipes* to support the buttocks, which explains Seneca's mention of "sitting on a cross."[385]

The only extant bones of a crucified man were discovered in Jerusalem in 1968 at Giv'at ha-Mivtar in a group of cave tombs dating from the second century B.C. to A.D. 70. A man named Jehohanan had been crucified sometime between A.D. 7 and 66.[386] Initial analysis suggested several possibilities that have later been refuted. (1) A scratch on the forearm near the wrist was interpreted to mean that he was nailed to the cross beam through the forearms. Thus it is possible that Jesus was not nailed to the cross through his palms, as Christian art has normally depicted it, but through the wrists or arms. The word translated "hands" in Luke 24:39 – 40 and John 20:20, 25, 27 may refer to wrist or arm.[387] Later analysis, however, has revealed that Jehohanan's arms and hands had not undergone violent injury, and it is more likely that he had been tied to the crossbeam with ropes.

Zugibe has determined that the upper part of the palm of the hand can support the weight of the body nailed to a cross.[388] It is therefore possible that tradition is correct, and Jesus was nailed to the cross through the palms of his hands.

(2) The iron nail piercing the man's heel bone had apparently hit a knot when it was driven into the cross and was bent, making it difficult to extract from the bone. The initial report suggested that this nail had been driven through both heels and that the man's legs were either pressed together and twisted so that the calves were parallel to the cross beam or possibly were spread apart. Later analysis showed that the nail was shorter than first described and was driven through the right heel, suggesting that the man had straddled the upright beam with each foot nailed laterally to the beam. Executioners employed a variety of ways of crucifying victims, and we cannot know precisely how Jesus was affixed to the cross.

(3) It was initially reported that the man's legs were fractured from a blow from a massive weapon shattering the right shin into slivers and fracturing the left one. This procedure was known as *crurifragium* and hastened death. According to the fictional *Gospel of Peter* 4:14, the people were angry with the penitent thief and did not allow his legs to be broken so that he would suffer longer. Later analysis of the bones, however, has questioned whether the man's legs had been broken.

Death by crucifixion normally came slowly and tortuously. Horace records a jeer that reflects this protracted suffering, "You'll hang on no cross to feed crows."[389] Seneca's letters offer gruesome images of crucifixion:

> Can anyone be found who would prefer wasting away in pain dying

**CRUCIFIED BONE**

The heel bone of a man crucified with an iron nail that pierced the bone and fastened him to the wood. The bone was found in an ossuary (burial box) in a Jerusalem tomb.

limb by limb, or letting out his life drop by drop, rather than expiring once for all? Can any man be found willing to be fastened to the accursed tree, long sickly, already deformed, swelling with ugly weals on shoulders and chest, and drawing the breath of life amid long drawn-out agony? He would have many excuses for dying even before mounting the cross.[390]

In another letter he writes:

> Yonder I see instruments of torture, not indeed of a single kind, but differently contrived by different peoples; some hang their victims with head toward the ground, some impale their private parts, others stretch out their arms on fork-shaped gibbet; I see cords, I see scourges, and for each separate limb and each joint there is a separate engine of torture.[391]

Reading this, one better understands the meaning of the word "excruciating," which derives from the Latin *excruciatus*, out of the cross.

**Dividing up his clothes, they cast lots to see what each would get (15:24).** Executioners customarily shared out the minor personal belongings of the condemned.[392] Not only does the victim suffer from the excruciating pain and thirst as well as the torture of insects burrowing into open wounds, he must also endure the humiliation of exposure. It is likely that Jesus was left with a loin cloth out of deference to Jewish scruples about nakedness.

**The written notice of the charge against him read: THE KING OF THE JEWS (15:26).** Jesus, who resisted any political overtones to his messiahship, is executed as a political Messiah. A placard citing the basic charge against him is probably hung around his neck as he departs for the execution site. To the Romans, any claim to kingship was treasonous.

**They crucified two robbers with him, one on his right and one on his left (15:27).** The robbers may have been involved in the insurrection with Barabbas (15:7), or they may be common thieves or bandits (11:17; see 2 Cor. 11:26).

**Those who passed by hurled insults at him (15:29).** Mocking a victim was customary and stemmed from the mob mentality of kicking a man when he is down. A rabbinic story tells of the crucifixion of Jose ben Joezer and the scorn hurled at him by his wicked nephew Jakum. He came up riding a horse on the Sabbath and mocked him: "Behold my horse which my master lets me ride and thy horse which thy Master (God) makes thee sit."[393] The "Aha" appears as a derisive cry in the Psalms, and the wagging of heads is a gesture of contempt.[394]

**At the sixth hour darkness came over the whole land until the ninth hour (15:33).** The darkness would have evoked several different images for ancient readers. (1) It was a sign of mourning (Jer. 4:27 – 28). According to a Talmudic tradition, when the president of the council dies, the sun is darkened; the rabbis comment that the sun mourns for the man even if humans do not.[395] (2) Darkness was associated in the ancient world with the death of great men. Philo saw the sun and moon as natural divinities and wrote that eclipses announce the death of kings and the destruction of cities.[396] Vergil wrote: "The Sun will give you signs. Who dare say the Sun is false? Nay, he oft warns us that dark uprisings threaten, that treachery and hidden wars are upswelling. Nay, he had pity for Rome when, after Caesar sank from sight, he veiled his shining face in dusky gloom, and a godless age feared everlasting night."[397] (3) In the Scriptures, darkness is an apocalyptic sign of judgment and could be construed as signaling the advent of divine judgment.[398] The darkness that descended during Jesus' crucifixion turns upside down the expectation derived from Isaiah 60:2 that though darkness covers the earth and dark night the nations, God's light will shine on Jerusalem. (4) The darkness also announces the great Day of the Lord in prophets such as Amos, and the darkness that settles on the land signifies that the day has dawned with a new beginning. (5) The darkness may veil the shame of the crucifixion: "God hides the Son from the blasphemer's leering."[399]

**"Eloi, Eloi, lama sabachthani?" — which means, "My God, my God, why have you forsaken me?" (15:34).** Jesus does not form the words of the prayer himself as he did in Gethsemane ("*Abba*"); rather, he cites a proverbial expression of distress from Psalm 22:1. One could not expect a crucifixion victim to recite an entire psalm, but it is possible that citing the first verse of the psalm refers to the entire psalm. Without chapters and verses to identify specific passages, initial words or key phrases were cited (see Mark 12:26). If this is the case here, Jesus prays the opening words of this lament psalm that, when read through to the end, expresses not only bitter despair but also supreme confidence. This interpretation does not deny the real anguish that Jesus experiences but understands his cry as an expression of trust that God will intervene and ultimately vindicate him.

**Listen, he's calling Elijah (15:35).** The final taunt arises from the popular belief that Elijah comes to aid those in mortal danger. According to a story in the Talmud, Elijah was said to have rescued one Eleazar ben Perata from the Romans and removed him four hundred miles away.[400]

**One man ran, filled a sponge with wine vinegar (15:36).** The name of this sour wine derives from the Greek word for sharp (*oxys*) and was made from water, egg, and vinegar. It was a soldier's drink. Marcus Cato was said to have called for it when he was in a raging thirst or when his strength was failing.[401] The one who went to get the wine may have hoped to give Jesus a spurt of energy to enable him to hold out until Elijah arrived.

**With a loud cry, Jesus breathed his last (15:37).** "Breathed out" (*ekpneueo*) is a rare word for death. Scholars have argued that death was caused by (1) a rupture of the heart; (2) asphyxiation as breathing became more difficult; or (3) shock from extreme physical punishment. From carefully conducted experiments, Zugibe refutes the asphyxiation theory and argues that Jesus' death was caused by traumatic shock from the effects of dehydration and loss of blood.[402]

**The curtain of the temple was torn in two from top to bottom (15:38).** Mark may refer to the outer curtain that separated the sanctuary from the outer porch[403] or to the inner veil between the Holy Place and the Most Holy Place.[404] The high priest on the Day of Atonement could go behind this veil into the Most Holy Place for only a brief moment. The veil was made of the finest wool — blue, purple, and scarlet; and, according to the Mishnah, was one handbreadth thick, forty cubits long, and twenty cubits broad and took three hundred priests to immerse it.[405] Josephus, a priest who would have firsthand knowledge of the veil, describes it as

> of Babylonian tapestry, with embroidery of blue and fine linen, of scarlet and also purple, wrought with marvelous skill. Nor was this mixture of materials without its mystic meaning: it typified the universe. For the scarlet seemed emblematical of fire, the fine linen of the earth, the blue of the air, and the purple of the sea; the comparison of the two cases being suggested by their colour, and in that of the fine linen and purple by their origin, as the one produced by the earth and the other by the sea. On this tapestry was portrayed a panorama of the heavens, the signs of the Zodiac excepted.[406]

The veil's rending may have both a negative and positive significance. Being torn from top to bottom points to its irremediable destruction and to God as the agent. It may signify the end of the Jewish cult and the destruction of the temple. Josephus records strange portents that he claimed gave early warning of the destruction that would later befall the temple. The massive, brass eastern gate of the temple's inner court took twenty men to close it every evening and fasten it shut with iron bars anchored to solid blocks of stone. Some years before the temple's destruction, it supposedly opened of its own accord.[407] The *Lives of the Prophets*, compiled by a Jew in the first century A.D. but preserved and edited by Christians, contains the following prophecy attributed to Habakkuk:

> And concerning the end of the Temple he predicted, "By a western nation it will happen." "At that time," he said, "the curtain of the *Dabeir* [transliteration of the Hebrew for the inner sanctuary, the Most Holy Place] will be torn into small pieces, and the capitals of the pillars will be removed and no one will know where they are" (12:12).

A Talmudic tradition also connects the rending of the veil with the temple's destruction. It records the Roman general Titus entering into the Most Holy Place and rending the veil with his sword, and blood poured out.[408]

The rending of the veil may also be interpreted as a decisive opening. All barriers between God and the people have now been removed (Heb. 10:19 – 20).

**And when the centurion, who stood there in front of Jesus, heard his cry and saw how he died, he said, "Surely this man was the Son of God!" (15:39).** Petronius, a courtier of Nero, recounts in his satiric novel, *Satyricon*, a soldier guarding the crosses of crucified thieves at night to prevent anyone from removing the bodies for burial.[409] It is probable that this was not the first crucifixion detail that the centurion had commanded. According to Mark, the centurion witnesses Jesus' death, not the rending of the veil. Consequently, we should not attempt to place the scene of the crucifixion at a spot where one might be able to see the veil being torn.

After Julius Caesar was deified, his adopted son, Augustus, became widely known as "son of god" (*divi filius*). It was not a title applied to emperors in general. This soldier transfers the title from the most revered figure in the Roman imperial cult to a Jew who has just been executed. The opening words of the Gospel (1:1) and this confession directly challenge the claims of the imperial cult. Jesus, not Augustus nor any other emperor, is Savior and Lord.[410]

**Some women were watching from a distance. Among them were Mary Magdalene, Mary the mother of James the younger and of Joses, and Salome (15:40).** Women customarily gathered in groups segregated from men. Magdalene suggests that Mary came from Magdala, three miles northeast of Tiberias and known as Taricheia in Greek. Church tradition says that she had been a prostitute, but there is no evidence in the New Testament for this.

**It was Preparation Day (15:42).** Mark explains that Preparation Day is the day preceding the Sabbath. Quitting all work on the Sabbath required much forethought and preparation. Before sunset, all business must be discharged, journeys ended, food prepared, and lamps fixed to burn longer since no light could be kindled on the Sabbath.

**Joseph of Arimathea, a prominent member of the Council, who was himself waiting for the kingdom of God, went boldly to Pilate and asked for Jesus' body (15:43).** The Romans frequently did not allow the bodies of executed persons to be taken down and buried.[411] Philo protested against the prefect Flaccus:

> On the eve of a holiday of this kind, people who have been crucified have been taken down and their bodies delivered to their kinsfolk, because it was thought well to give them burial and allow ordinary rites. For it was meet that the dead also should have the advantage of some kind treatment upon the birthday of an emperor and also that the sanctity of the festival should be maintained.

Flaccus gave no orders to take down the bodies of the executed Jews but crucified more instead.[412]

Deuteronomy 21:22–23 became the basis for the Jewish belief that one was obligated to bury the body of criminals and even enemies on the day of their death. Philo paraphrases the text, "Let not the sun go down upon the crucified but let them be buried in the earth before sundown."[413] Josephus writes about the treacherous attack of the Idumeans in the first revolt when they killed the chief priests and refused to allow them to be buried: "They actually went so far as to cast out the corpses without burial, although the Jews are so careful about funeral rites that even the malefactors who have been sentenced to crucifixion are taken down and buried before sunset."[414]

Arimathea may designate that Joseph comes from Ramathaim (1 Sam. 1:1), east of Joppa, or Rathamin to the northwest (1 Macc. 11:34). He is described as someone of high standing and noble repute. He may have been a member of his local ruling body or a member of the council that decided Jesus deserved death. Why would he then wish to claim the body? Joseph is described with emphasis as looking for the kingdom of God, which identifies him as a pious man (see the description of Simeon and Anna, Luke 2:25, 38). The statement that it is already the evening of the Preparation Day, the day before Sabbath (Mark 15:42), provides the motivation for why he wishes to act and act quickly. A body must not be allowed to hang beyond sundown into the Sabbath. Joseph fulfills the pious obligation to bury the dead and thus prevents a body left on the cross from affronting God and defiling the land and the Sabbath (Deut. 21:23).

If Joseph is not a follower of Jesus at this point, it may explain why the women do not come near and assist in the burial but watch from a distance. In Acts 8:2, when Stephen was stoned, pious men, *not* Christians, buried him and made great lamentation over him. Regarding Jesus' burial, Acts 13:29 asserts that when "they had carried out all that was written of him, they took him down from the tree and laid him in a tomb." The context implies that enemies of Jesus buried him.

Ordinarily, family or friends requested the body of one who was executed (see the disciples of John the Baptist, 6:29). Yet Jesus' disciples do not do this. That Joseph "went boldly" to ask Pilate for the body suggests that the request involved some risk. Jesus has been executed for treason as the king of the Jews. To ask for the body of one guilty of *maiestas* could be looked upon as sympathizing.

In Matthew 27:57, Joseph is identified as a disciple and rich. The aorist verb, however, may be translated that he became a disciple at a later time and need not mean that he was counted among the disciples when he buried Jesus. In Luke 23:50 – 51, he is identified as a good and righteous man, who did not consent to their plan and action and who was waiting for the kingdom of God. In John 19:38, he is identified as a secret disciple. Possibly, Joseph became a follower of Jesus after the resurrection, which explains why his name was remembered in the tradition.

**So Joseph bought some linen cloth, took down the body, wrapped it in the linen, and placed it in a tomb cut out of rock (15:46).** "Some linen cloth" translates the word *sindon* (see 14:51 – 52). It may refer to pieces of cloth to wrap the body but more likely refers to a single piece of linen cloth not unlike the spurious Shroud of Turin.

The surviving tombs from this period appear to belong to wealthier families. Most of the population apparently were buried in "simple shallow pits" that have not survived.[415] Wealthier Jews practiced secondary burial. When the flesh had decomposed, the bones were carefully gathered up and placed in an ossuary box,

**ROCK-HEWN TOMBS**

Examples of Roman-era rolling stone tombs in Israel.

▼

# TOMB OF JOSEPH AND THE EDICULE

Looking at the present edicule, it is impossible to know what the original tomb of Jesus looked like. We can now reconstruct that original by comparison with 63 other round-stone tombs from the time of Christ. Probably the closest of these 63 would be Heshbon Tomb F.1 which of all 63 most closely follows the plan found in the Mishnah Baba Bathiza 6:8. This form temporarily died out at A.D. 70 with the Roman destruction, but was brought back in the 4th century A.D.

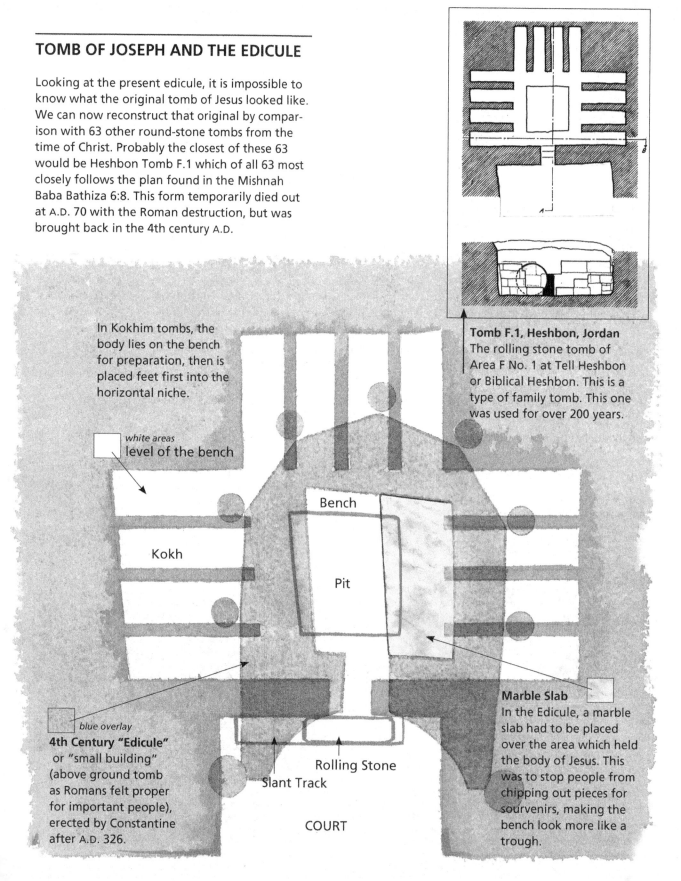

**Tomb F.1, Heshbon, Jordan**
The rolling stone tomb of Area F No. 1 at Tell Heshbon or Biblical Heshbon. This is a type of family tomb. This one was used for over 200 years.

In Kokhim tombs, the body lies on the bench for preparation, then is placed feet first into the horizontal niche.

*white areas*
level of the bench

Kokh

Bench

Pit

*blue overlay*
**4th Century "Edicule"** or "small building" (above ground tomb as Romans felt proper for important people), erected by Constantine after A.D. 326.

Slant Track

Rolling Stone

COURT

**Marble Slab**
In the Edicule, a marble slab had to be placed over the area which held the body of Jesus. This was to stop people from chipping out pieces for sourvenirs, making the bench look more like a trough.

the larger bones on the bottom and smaller bones on top. This practice allowed tombs to be reused. The coffin-less body would be placed in a niche (*kokh*, up to 2 ft wide and 7 ft deep) cut horizontally into the wall of the tomb chamber. Another type of tomb had trough-like shelves hewn along the sides of the chamber with an arched ceiling (*acrosolinium*). A third type of tomb had a low bench cut around three sides of the chamber. Mark's account of the angel sitting inside on the right (16:5) seems to describe a tomb with a bench, and John 20:6, 8 suggests it has an anteroom.

**Then he rolled a stone against the entrance of the tomb (15:46).** The tombs in this period had small, low openings into cave-like chambers that were closed with stone blocks (see John 11:38 – 39) or with rolling stones (like a mill stone) in slanted tracks. Sealing the tomb prevented the body from being disturbed and shut out dirt. But it also shut down its potential defiling effects. A tomb with a door was ruled as not spreading defilement on all sides, and one could safely walk above it without being defiled.

A discussion in the *Tosepta* describes the case of a man who died on the eve of Passover. To bury him, the women tied a rope to the rolling stone and the men pulled on the rope from outside to move it. The women then entered the tomb and buried the man. By not touching directly the body or the rolling stone, the men remained in a state of purity and were able to eat the Passover.[416]

The tomb in which Jesus was laid had to be nearby since the body had to be buried quickly before the Sabbath. Visitors to Jerusalem are frequently shown the garden tomb, discovered in 1867, as the site of Jesus' burial. It is a more peaceful and picturesque locale than the Holy Sepulchre church and definitely outside the city wall. The archaeological evidence, however, rules it out, since it was hewn in Iron Age II (eighth to seventh century B.C.). No other tombs that can be dated to the time of Jesus have been uncovered in this area, and it differs from other excavated burial caves that date from the first century.[417]

## The Report of the Resurrection (16:1 – 8)

**When the Sabbath was over, Mary Magdalene, Mary the mother of James, and Salome bought spices so that they might go to anoint Jesus' body (16:1).** It was customary to check a tomb before three days to make sure that the person was dead. "After the Sabbath" explains why the women do not come to the tomb sooner; they do not want to violate the Sabbath.

Anointing a body with aromatic oils neutralized the smell from its decomposition, and sometimes anointing the body was repeated. Gundry contends that Jews customarily used oil, not aromatics, and argues that the burial of a king was the exception (see 2 Chron. 16:14; Song 4:10).[418] The dignity of anointing Jesus' body with spices is an attempt to remove the disgrace of the crucifixion for the Son of God, who deserves no less than a king. The women may have judged that what Joseph did was insufficient.

**Who will roll the stone away from the entrance of the tomb? (16:3).** Stones required some force to move them back along the sloped groove. The entrance would have been small and one needed to stoop to enter, but the inner court would have been high enough for one to stand.

As they entered the tomb, they saw a young man dressed in a white robe sitting on the right side (16:5). The white robe is the characteristic dress of heavenly beings.[419] Angels were not pictured with wings. Only the seraphim had wings, and they numbered six (Isa. 6:2). Cherubim had animal and human features, but the Bible describes angels as quite human-like.[420] In 2 Maccabees 3:26, angels are described as "two young men . . . remarkably strong, gloriously beautiful and splendidly dressed." Josephus describes the angel who appears to Manoah's wife (Judg. 13:13) "as being in the likeness of a beautiful youth."[421]

**Don't be alarmed (16:6).** Angels typically urge those to whom they appear not to be afraid or amazed.[422]

**They said nothing to anyone, because they were afraid (16:8).** The earliest and most reliable texts conclude Mark's gospel at 16:8. This abrupt ending has caused consternation for many, however. How could a Gospel end on a note of apparent failure and with no resurrection appearances? Two other existing endings to Mark's Gospel testify to early dissatisfaction or an uneasiness with this finale. (1) A shorter ending, extant in only a handful of later manuscripts, is clearly a subsequent attempt to tie up the loose ends. The phrase "the sacred and imperishable proclamation of eternal salvation" plainly derives from the church's language of a later era.

(2) A better-attested longer ending (16:9 – 20), recording three appearances of Jesus and his ascension, contains vocabulary and style that differ noticeably from that found in the rest of Mark. The transition from verse 8 to verse 9 is rough, suddenly switching to Jesus'

appearing to Mary Magdalene and completely ignoring the other two women. Mary Magdalene was introduced in 15:40, 47 and 16:1 without any further description, but she now is identified as the one out of whom Jesus cast out seven demons (see Luke 8:2). Careful analysis points to a later scribe in the second century reworking accounts from the other Gospels or oral traditions to compose a more reassuring ending for Mark.

Speculations about a lost ending or suggestions that Mark somehow may have failed to complete his Gospel are not helpful. Mark may have felt no need to relate resurrection appearances already familiar to his readers. The Gospel begins as abruptly as it ends, and it is more likely that Mark intends this suspenseful ending to provoke a reaction in the reader. The reader knows the disciples eventually reunite with Jesus in story time if not in the plotted time of the Gospel; otherwise, this Gospel would never have been written. Paul says he reminded the Corinthians that he related these events to them as of first importance (1 Cor. 15:3 – 5). The word of Jesus' resurrection has clearly been made public. The repetition of Jesus' prediction that they will meet him in Galilee (Mark 16:7; cf. 14:28) also guarantees that these things do come to pass, because the other predictions he made in the Passion Narrative were fulfilled to the letter.

Since Mark does not narrate how this reunion occurs, the reader can only conclude that God overrode human fear, failure, and disobedience to accomplish it — as God always does. One must infer that success does not depend on the heroism of individual believers, whose flesh is weak and whose spirit is not always willing, but on the power of God.

## ANNOTATED BIBLIOGRAPHY

France, R. T. *Divine Government: God's Kingship in the Gospel of Mark.* London: SPCK, 1990.

A compelling overview of a key theme in Mark.

Garland, David E. *Mark.* NIVAC. Grand Rapids: Zondervan, 1996.

A commentary that combines analysis of the original meaning of the text with discussion of how to bridge the contexts to our world and make contemporary application.

Geddert, Timothy J. *Watchwords: Mark 13 in Markan Eschatology.* JSNTSup 26. Sheffield: JSOT, 1989.

A brilliantly conceived dissertation that is not only readable but offers keen insights into the text of Mark.

Gundry, Robert H. *Mark: A Commentary on His Apology for the Cross.* Grand Rapids: Eerdmans, 1993.

A carefully argued commentary with extensive interaction with the technical scholarship on Mark.

Hooker, Morna D. *The Gospel According to Saint Mark.* BNTC. Peabody, Mass.: Hendrickson, 1991.

A more popular commentary by an astute interpreter of Mark.

Juel, Donald. *A Master of Surprise.* Philadelphia: Fortress, 1994.

An excellent overview of the Gospel.

Lane, William L. *Commentary on the Gospel of Mark.* NICNT. Grand Rapids: Eerdmans, 1974.

One of the classic commentaries on Mark that has stood well the test of time.

Schweizer, Eduard. *The Good News According to Mark.* Richmond, Va.: John Knox, 1970.

A scintillating treatment of Mark by a renown biblical scholar.

# CHAPTER NOTES

## Main Text Notes

1. See also Col. 4:10; Philem. 24; 1 Peter 5:13.
2. Tacitus, *Hist.* 1.2–3.
3. Joel Marcus, *The Way of the Lord: Christological Exegesis of the Old Testament in the Gospel of Mark* (Louisville: Westminster/John Knox, 1992), 76.
4. See Gen. 6:2; Job 1:6; 2:1; 38:7; Ps. 82:6; Dan. 3:25.
5. See Ex. 4:22–23; Deut. 1:31; 14:1; 32:5–6; Jer. 31:9, 20; Hos. 11:1; see also Wisd. Sol. 18:13; *Jub. 1:24–25; T. Mos.* 10:3; *Pss. Sol.* 17:27; 18:4; *Sib. Or.* 3:702.
6. See Wisd. Sol. 2:18; Sir. 4:10; compare Matt. 5:9.
7. *Jos. Asen.* 6:3, 5; 13:10; 21:3; 23:10.
8. 2 Sam. 7:14; Ps. 2:7; cf. 89:26–27.
9. See *4 Ezra* 7:28–29; 13:32, 37, 52; 14:9; 4QFlor 1:11–13; 1Qsa 2:11–12; *1 En.* 105:2; see also *b. Sukkah* 52a. Later Judaism would have expunged such usage because of Christian use of the title for Jesus.
10. Adolf Deissmann, *Light from the Ancient East* (1922; reprint, Grand Rapids: Baker, 1978), 295.
11. Robert H. Gundry, *Mark: A Commentary on His Apology for the Cross* (Grand Rapids: Eerdmans, 1993), 34.
12. Mark characteristically fuses Scripture, see 1:11 (Isa. 42:1/Ps. 2:7); 11:1–11 (Zech. 9:9/Ps. 118:25–26); 11:17 (Isa. 56:7/Jer. 7:11); 12:1–12 (Isa. 5:1–2/Ps. 118:22–23); 13:24–26 (Isa. 13:10/34:4/Ezek. 32:7–8/Joel 2:10); 14:62 (Dan. 7:13/Ps. 110:1).
13. Marcus, *The Way of the Lord*, 20.
14. Ex. 2:15; 1 Sam. 23:14; 1 Kings 19:3–4.
15. See 2 Macc. 5:27; Philo, *Decalogue* 1.2.
16. 1QS 8:13–14.
17. *b. Ker.* 9a; 81a; *b. Yebam.* 46a; see 1 Cor. 10:2.
18. Ezek. 36:25–27; see also Isa. 4:3–4; Zech. 13:1; 1QS 4:20–21.
19. *m. Miqw.* 8:5; 9:1.
20. Josephus, *Ant.* 18.5.2 § 117.
21. 2 Kings 1:8; see Zech. 13:4.
22. Gustav Dalman, *Sacred Sites and Ways*, trans. Paul P. Levortoff (New York: Macmillan, 1935), 84.
23. Josephus, *J.W.* 4.8.3 § 469.
24. *Mekilta Nezikin* 1 to Ex. 21:2; *Mekilta de-Rabbi Ishmael* trans. Jacob Z. Lauterbach (Philadelphia: Jewish Publications Society of America, 1935), 3:5–6.
25. See Ezek. 1:1; 3; John 1:51; Acts 7:56; Rev. 4:1; 11:19; 19:11.
26. Josephus, *Ant.* 20.5.1 §97.
27. *b. Ḥag.* 15a.
28. F. E. Greenspahn, "Why Prophesy Ceased," *JBL* 108 (1989): 37–49.
29. *y. Soṭah* 13:2.
30. The same verb occurs in Mark 3:19; 9:31; 10:33; 14:10, 11, 18, 21, 41, 42, 44; 15:1, 10, 15.
31. See *4 Ezra* 4:36–37; 9:5; 11:44; *2 Bar.* 40:3.
32. Charles R. Page II, *Jesus and the Land* (Nashville: Abingdon, 1995), 73.
33. Mendel Nun, *The Sea of Galilee and Its Fishermen in the New Testament* (Tiberias: En Gev, 1989); John J. Rousseau and Rami Arav, *Jesus and His World: An Archaeological and Cultural Dictionary* (Minneapolis: Fortress, 1995), 94; K. C. Hanson, "The Galilean Fishing Economy and the Jesus Tradition," *BTB* 27 (1997): 105.
34. Jer. 16:14–16; Ezek. 29:4; 32:3; Amos 4:2; Hab. 1:14–17.
35. *Jos. Asen.* 21:21.
36. James F. Strange and Hershel Shanks, "Synagogue Where Jesus Preached Found at Capernaum," *BAR* 9 (1983): 24–31.
37. Daniel K. Falk, "Jewish Prayer Literature and the Jerusalem Church in Acts," in *The Book of Acts in Its First Century Setting; vol. 4 of Palestinian Setting*, ed. Richard Bauckham (Grand Rapids: Eerdmans, 1995), 282.
38. Sherman E. Johnson, *Jesus and His Towns* (GNS 29; Wilmington Del.: Michael Glazier, 1989), 69.
39. G. B. Caird, *New Testament Theology*, ed. L. D. Hurst (Oxford: Clarendon, 1994), 109.
40. William L. Lane, *Commentary on the Gospel of Mark* (NICNT; Grand Rapids: Eerdmans, 1974), 74, citing O. Bauernfeind, *Die Worte der Dämonen in Markusevangelium* (Stuttgart, 1927).
41. *m. Demai* 3:6.
42. See John Granger Cook, "In Defense of Ambiguity: Is There a Hidden Demon in Mark 1.29–31?" *NTS* 43 (1997): 184–208.
43. *b. Ned.* 41a.
44. Bargil Pixner, *With Jesus through Galilee According to the Fifth Gospel* (Collegeville: Liturgical, 1992), 34.
45. *m. Neg.* 1:1.
46. *m. Neg.* 3:1; 4:7–10; *t. Meg.* 1:1.
47. Lev. 13:45–52; Num. 5:2–4.
48. The interpretations of the rabbis argued that one became defiled by a leper by passing under a tree where a leper was standing (*m. Neg.* 13:7; *b. Ber.* 25a), entering a leprous house (*b. Ber.* 41a), or being in a house which a leper entered (*m. Neg.* 13:11; *m. Kel.* 1:4).
49. *m. Neg.* 13:12; *t. Neg.* 7:11.

50. *Lev. Rab.* 16:3.
51. M. Wojciechowski, "The Touching of the Leper (Mark 1,40–45) as a Historical and Symbolic Act of Jesus," *BZ* 33 (1989): 114–119.
52. Morna D. Hooker, *The Gospel According to Saint Mark* (BNTC; Peabody, Mass.: Hendrickson, 1991), 79.
53. Rousseau and Arav, *Jesus and His World*, 340.
54. 4Q242.
55. *b. Ned.* 41a.
56. *b. Meg.* 17b.
57. See the paralysis of Alcimus in 1 Macc. 9:55, and of Ptolemy IV Philopator in *3 Macc.* 2:21–23.
58. See Isa. 33:24; Jer. 31:34; and Mic. 7:18.
59. 2 Sam. 12:13; Isa. 6:7; 43:25; 44:22.
60. 1 Sam. 16:7; 1 Chron. 28:9; Ps. 139:1–2, 6, 23; Jer. 11:20; 17:9–10; Acts 1:24.
61. *m. Ned.* 3:4.
62. Plutarch, *On Curiosity* 518E.
63. Josephus, *J.W.* 2.14.4 § 287; 2.14.5 § 292.
64. See Acts 16:34; *Jos. Asen.* 20:8.
65. John Riches, *Jesus and the Transformation of Judaism* (New York: Seabury, 1982), 105.
66. See, e.g., Ps. 1:1, "Blessed is the man who does not walk in the counsel of the wicked or stand in the way of sinners or sit in the seat of mockers."
67. *Mekilta Amalek* 3 to Ex. 18:1.
68. Gundry, *Mark*, 129.
69. Lev. 16:29, 31; 23:27, 32; Num. 29:7.
70. 1 Sam. 31:13; 2 Sam. 1:12; 3:35; 12:21; 1 Kings 21:27; Est. 4:3; Ps. 35:13–14; 69:10; Isa. 58:5; Jonah 3:5.
71. Isa. 62:5; Ezek. 16:7–14; see Isa. 54:4–8.
72. *m. Šabb.* 7:2.
73. See Judith 8:6; *Jub.* 50:2; *m. Taʿan.* 1:6.
74. Ps. 137:5; Zech. 11:17.
75. CD 11:10; *m. Šabb.* 14:3–4; *t. Šabb.* 12:8–14.
76. *t. Šabb.* 16:22; *b. Šabb.* 12a.
77. *m. Yoma* 8:6; *Mekilta Shabbata* 1 to Ex. 31:12.
78. Josephus, *Ant.* 15.10.4–5 §§ 371–79.
79. Otto Betz, "Jesus and the Temple Scroll," *Jesus and the Dead Sea Scrolls*, ed. J. H. Charlesworth (New York: Doubleday, 1992), 76–78.
80. Num. 1:1–19, 44; see also Gen. 49:28.
81. See Gen. 17:5, 15; 32:28.
82. Chrys C. Caragounis, *Peter and the Rock* (BZNW 58; Berlin/New York: Walter de Gruyter, 1990), 12, 15.
83. *b. Sanh.* 43a. See also *b. Sanh.* 107b; *t. Šabb.* 11:15; John 7:20; 8:48, 52; 10:20.
84. Num. 15:30–31; 1 Sam. 3:14; Isa. 22:14.
85. Alan Hugh McNeile, *The Gospel According to St. Matthew* (London: Macmillan, 1915), 179.
86. C. E. B. Cranfield, *The Gospel According to St. Mark* (CGTC; Cambridge: Cambridge Univ. Press, 1966), 159.
87. R. T. France, *Divine Government: God's Kingship in the Gospel of Mark* (London: SPCK, 1990), 30.
88. Seneca, *Mor. Ep.* 38.2; 73.16; Quintilian, 5.11.24; Burton L. Mack and Vernon K. Robbins, *Patterns of Persuasion in the Gospels* (Sonoma: Polebridge, 1989), 156.
89. Mack and Robbins, *Patterns of Persuasion in the Gospels*, 156.
90. Jer. 31:27–28; Ezek. 36:9; Hos. 2:21–23; *4 Ezra* 9:31; see Mark 3:20.
91. See Ezek. 36:9; Hos. 10:11–12; *Jub.* 11:11.
92. K. D. White, "The Parable of the Sower," *JTS* 15 (1964): 304.
93. Pliny, *Nat. Hist.* 18.21.94–95. Varro said seed in Syria could yield a hundred fold (*On Agriculture* 2.9.5–6).
94. John H. Martin, Warren H. Leonard, and David L. Stamp, *Principles of Field Crop Production* (New York: Macmillan, 1976), 436.
95. Strabo, *Geogr.* (SBL 261) 15.3.11.
96. Job 15:8; Ps. 25:14; Prov. 3:32; Amos 3:7.
97. 1QS 5:11.
98. See *Jub.* 11:5–24; *b. Sanh.* 107a.
99. Jer. 25:10; Matt. 25:1–13; Rev. 18:22–23.
100. *b. Ber.* 40a.
101. *m. Nidda* 5:2; *m. Nazir* 1:5; *m. Tohar.* 8:8.
102. Claus-Hunno Hunzinger, "σίναπι," TDNT, 7.289.
103. Charles E. Carlston, *The Parables of the Triple Tradition* (Philadelphia: Fortress, 1975), 162.
104. Pliny, *Nat. Hist.* 19:170–71.
105. Gundry, *Mark*, 267.
106. See Ps. 104:12, 16–17.
107. *1 En.* 90:30, 33, 37; *Midr. Ps.* 104:10.
108. 1QH 6:14–17; 8:4–8.
109. Luke 5:1; "Sea of Kinnereth," Num. 34:11; Josh. 12:3; 13:27.
110. Pixner, *Galilee*, 89. See Josephus, *J.W.* 3.10.7 § 515.
111. Shelley Wachsmann, *The Sea of Galilee Boat: An Extraordinary 200 Year Old Discovery* (New York: Plenum, 1995), 349; Hanson, "The Galilean Fishing Economy," 106.
112. Rousseau and Arav, *Jesus and His World*, 246.
113. Page, *Jesus and the Land*, 183, n. 30.
114. See also Ps. 69:1–2; 89:9–10; 104:7.
115. See also Ps. 104:7; 106:9; Isa. 50:2; Nah. 1:4.
116. Ps. 3:5; 4:8; 46:1–3; Prov. 3:23–26.
117. See Job 30:6; Heb. 11:38; *b. Ber.* 3b; *b. Šabb.* 67a; *b. Giṭ.* 70a; *b. Sanh.* 65b.
118. Cf. Str-B 1.491–92.
119. *T. Sol.* 5:1–13; 13:1–17. See *PGM* 1.160–61 for asking a demon to divulge its name: "What is your divine name? Reveal it to me ungrudgingly, so that I may call upon it."

120. Matt. 12:43; Luke 11:24; see also Tobit 8:3.

121. 1 Macc. 1:62–64; 2 Macc 6:18–7:42.

122. Josephus, *J.W.* 3.7.31 § 289.

123. Pliny, *Nat. Hist.* 7.64.

124. Noted by Jacob Milgrom, *Leviticus 1–16* (AB; New York: Doubleday, 1991), 948.

125. Josephus reports that the temple was closed to women during their menstruation (*J.W.* 5.5.6 § 227; *Ag. Ap.* 2.8 §§103–4).

126. See 2 Chron. 16:12; Job 13:4; Jer. 46:11; 51:8; and Philo, *Sacrifices* 70–71.

127. *t. B. Bat.* 10:6.

128. *m. Qidd.* 4:14.

129. *b. Pesah.* 113a.

130. *b. Šabb.* 110a.

131. John P. Meier, *A Marginal Jew: Rethinking the Historical Jesus* (New York: Doubleday, 1991), 1.785.

132. An inscription shows that Nazareth was spelled with the Hebrew letter tzade (Pixner, *Galilee*, 15).

133. *Jos. Asen.* 6:10.

134. Meier, *A Marginal Jew*, 1.281.

135. Origen, *Contra Celsum* 6.36.

136. Richard Bauckham, "The Brothers and Sisters of Jesus: An Epiphanian Response to John P. Meier," *CBQ* 56 (1994): 698–700.

137. Josephus also refers to James as "the brother of Jesus" (*Ant.* 20.9.1 § 200).

138. Num. 35:30; Deut. 17:6; 19:15; 2 Cor. 13:1; 1 Tim. 5:19.

139. André Parrott, *Land of Christ: Archaeology, History, Geography* (Philadelphia: Fortress, 1968), 48–49.

140. See also Ex. 12:11; Ezek. 20:37; 37:15–28.

141. *m. ʾOhal.* 2:3; *m. Tehar.* 4:5.

142. Philo, *Dreams* 2.58.

143. Josephus, *Ant.* 18.5.2 § 119.

144. Josephus, *J.W.* 7.6.2 §§ 171–77.

145. Josephus, *Ant.* 18.5.1 §§ 109–15.

146. Ibid., 18.5.2 §118.

147. Compare the story of the pledge of the emperor Gaius to Agrippa (Josephus *Ant.* 18.8.7 §§ 289–304).

148. Vincent Taylor, *The Gospel According to St Mark* (London: Macmillan, 1966), 311.

149. *m. ʿAbod. Zar.* 1:3.

150. The story of another dancing girl appears in Josephus, *Ant.* 12.5.6 §§186–89.

151. The dimensions of a loaf according to *m. Peʾah* 8:7. It probably looked somewhat like modern pita bread.

152. See Ex. 18:21, 25 (officers over thousands, hundreds, fifties, and tens); 1QS 2:21–22; 1QSa 1:14–15, 27–2:1; 2:11–22; 1QM 4:1–5:16; CD 13:1.

153. Josephus, *Life* §§ 398–406.

154. Josephus, *Ant.* 18.2.1 § 28; but see idem *J.W.* 2.9.1 § 168, which seems to connect it

to the wife of Augustus, Livia (given the name Julia after her death in 29 B.C.), instead of his daughter, who had been discredited. Her third marriage in 11 B.C. to Tiberius, the stepson of Augustus, ended in estrangement; and her father exiled her for her adulteries in 2 B.C. On this issue, see Fred Strickert, *Bethsaida: Home of the Apostles* (Collegeville, Minn.: Liturgical, 1998), 91–107.

155. Ibid., 41–45.

156. Job 9:8; 38:8–11; Prov. 8:29; Isa. 43:16; 51:10; Hab. 3:15; Sir. 24:5–6.

157. See Ex. 33:19–23; 34:5–6; 1 Kings 19:11; Job 9:8, 11 (see LXX; "He walks upon the waves of the sea. . . If he goes by me, I will not see him, and if he passes by me, I will not recognize him"); Dan 12:1 (LXX) describing the glory of the Lord passing by; Amos 7:8; 8:22.

158. Ex. 3:14; Deut. 32:39; Isa. 41:2–14; 43:1–13 (cf. v. 2, "When you pass through the waters I will be with you"); 44:1–5; 46:4; 48:12; 51:9–16; 52:6.

159. *b. B. Bat.* 73a; cited by Lane, *Mark*, 237.

160. Josephus, *J.W.* 3.10.7–8 §§506, 516–21.

161. Yigael Yadin, *Bar-Kokhba* (London: Weidenfeld and Nicolson, 1978), 81–85.

162. Deut. 12:15, 22; 15:22.

163. Lev. 15:7; 16:26, 28; 17:15–16; 22:1–7.

164. Josephus, *J.W.* 2.8.5 § 129.

165. *Let. of Aris.* 305–6.

166. *b. Ber.* 60b.

167. *m. ʾAbot* 1:1–2.

168. Josephus, *J.W.* 2.8.10 § 150.

169. See *b. Ber.* 47b.

170. See Prov. 28:24; 1 Tim. 5:4.

171. *b. Qidd.* 31b.

172. Josephus considers it to be a distinctive Jewish oath, see *Ant.* 4.4.4 § 73; *Ag. Ap.* 1.166–67.

173. *m. Ned.* 5:6.

174. *m. Makš.* 6:7; *t. Miqw.* 7:8.

175. *y. Pesah.* 7:11.

176. According to *Sifra Mes. Zab.* 1:12–13.

177. See Josephus *J.W.* 2.8.9 §§ 148–49; 1QM 7:3–7; 11QT 46:15–16. See further the discussion in Harrington, *Impurity Systems of Qumran*, 100–103.

178. Josephus, *Ag. Ap.* 1.70. See also Isa. 23; Jer. 25:22; 27:3; 47:4; Ezek. 26–28; Joel 3:4; Amos 1:9; Zech. 9:2. In Matt. 11:21–24, Tyre and Sidon are equivalent to Sodom and Gomorrah.

179. Martin Hengel, *Studies in the Gospel of Mark* (London: SCM, 1985), 29.

180. Deut. 32:6; Isa. 1:2; Jer. 31:9; Hos. 11:1; Rom. 9:4.

181. *m. ʾAbot* 3:15.

**111**

**Mark**

182. See 1 Sam. 17:43; 24:14; 2 Sam. 3:8; 9:8; 16:9; 2 Kings 8:13; Prov. 26:11; Eccl. 9:4; Isa. 56:10–11; *m. Pesah.* 8:8.

183. *b. Ḥag.* 13a.

184. *Jos. Asen.* 10:13.

185. Gerd Theissen, *The Gospels in Context: Social and Political History in the Synoptic Tradition* (Minneapolis: Fortress, 1991), 61–80.

186. See Sean Freyne, *Galilee: From Alexander the Great to Hadrian 323 BCE to 135 CE* (Edinburgh: T. & T. Clark, 1980), 8, 117–21.

187. See Ezek. 26:1–27:36; Joel 3:4–21; Amos 1:9–10; Zech. 9:1–4.

188. Suetonius, *Vespasian* 8:7.

189. Juvenal, *Sat.* 3.14; 6.542.

190. Jeffrey B. Gibson, "Jesus' Refusal to Produce a 'Sign' (Mark 8.11–13)," *JSNT* 38 (1990): 53.

191. Plutarch, *Roman Questions* 289F; see also Pliny, *Nat. Hist.* 18.26.

192. Pliny, *Nat. Hist.* 28.37.

193. Francis Watson, "Ambiguity in the Marcan Narrative," *KTR* 10 (1987): 12.

194. Josephus, *Ant.* 15.10.3 § 364.

195. Ibid., 15.10.3 § 364; idem, *J.W.* 1.21.3 §§ 404–5.

196. Josephus, *Ant.* 18.2.1 § 28; *J.W.* 2.9.1 § 168.

197. Lane, *Mark*, 288.

198. Gen. 22:4; Hos. 6:2; cf. Jonah 2:1.

199. Lane, *Mark*, 296.

200. 1QS 2:13–14; 6:14–15; 10:12–13; 1QH 9:23.

201. Clarence E. Glad, "Frank Speech, Flattery, and Friendship in Philodemus," in *Friendship, Flattery and Frankness of Speech: Studies on Friendship in the New Testament World*, ed. John T. Fitzgerald, (NovTSup 82; Leiden: Brill, 1996), 42.

202. Plutarch, *Moralia* 554A/B.

203. Dionysius of Halicarnassus, *Roman Antiquities* 7.69.1–2.

204. Josephus *J.W.* 4.1.8. §§ 54–61.

205. See Dan. 12:3; Matt. 13:43; Rev. 7:13–14; *1 En.* 38:4; 58:3; 62:15–16; 104:2; *2 En.* 22:8; 66:7; *2 Apoc. Bar.* 51:1–3, 10, 12.

206. Randall E. Otto, "The Fear Motivation in Peter's Offer to Build τρεῖς σκηνάς," *WTJ* 59 (1997): 105.

207. Wayne A. Meeks, *The Prophet-King: Moses Traditions and the Johannine Christology* (Leiden: Brill, 1967), 124; Marcus, *The Way of the Lord*, 89.

208. *Deut. Rab.* 3:17.

209. Otto, "The Fear Motivation in Peter's Offer," 106.

210. Ibid., 104.

211. *m. ʿEd.* 8:7; *m. Šeqal.* 2:5; *m. B. Mesiʿa* 1:8.

212. Justin Martyr, *Dialogue With Rabbi Trypho* 8.4; 49.1.

213. John J. Pilch, *The Cultural World of Jesus* (Collegeville: Liturgical, 1996), 30.

214. Josephus, *J.W.* 7.6.3 § 185.

215. Acts 13:2; 14:23; *Did.* 7; 8; Justin, *Apology* 61.

216. *b. Nid.* 13b.

217. Deut. 14:1; 1 Kings 18:28; Zech. 13:6.

218. 2 Chron. 28:3; 33:6; Jer. 7:31–32.

219. 2 Kings 2:21–22; Ezek. 16:4; 43:24.

220. *Sib. Or.* 2:252–55.

221. *m. ʿArak.* 5:6; see also *m. Yebam.* 14:1.

222. Josephus, *Life* § 427.

223. *m. Ketub.* 4:9.

224. *m. Giṭ.* 6:2.

225. *b. Yebam.* 63b.

226. Michael O. Wise, *A Critical Study of the Temple Scroll from Cave 11* (Chicago: Oriental Institute of the Univ. of Chicago, 1990), 161–75. See 11Q Temple 57:11–19; CD 4:18–21.

227. Josephus, *Ant.* 15.7.10 § 259.

228. Ibid., 20.7.2 §§ 141–43.

229. Ibid., 18.5.4. § 136.

230. Malina and Rohrbaugh, *Social-Science Commentary on the Synoptic Gospels*, 243.

231. Ibid., 244.

232. Martin Hengel, *Poverty and Riches in the Early Church* (Philadelphia: Fortress, 1974), 8. See *m. ʿArak.* 8:4; *b. Ketub.* 50a; *b. Taʿan.* 24a.

233. G. W. E. Nickelsburg, "Riches in 1 Enoch 92–95," *NTS* 25 (1979): 327. See also Bruce J. Malina, "Wealth and Poverty in the New Testament," *Int* 41 (1987): 361; *The New Testament World: Insights from Cultural Anthropology* (Atlanta: John Knox, 1981), 75–85. See also Sir. 13:3–4; 34:20–22.

234. See *Jos. Asen.* 10:11–13. On Asenath's conversion, she threw all her goods out her palace window for the poor and the beggars.

235. *b. Ber.* 55b; *b. B. Mesiʿa* 38b.

236. See P. S. Minear, "The Needle's Eye: A Study in Form Criticism," *JBL* 61 (1942): 157–69.

237. See Job 1:10; 42:10; Ps. 128:1–2; Isa. 3:10.

238. Tacitus, *Hist.* 2.59.

239. Ps. 75:8; Isa. 51:17, 22; Jer. 25:15, 28; 49:12.

240. Plato, *Gorgias* 491E.

241. Seneca, *On Benefits* 3.19.1.

242. Ex. 21:30; Lev. 25:51–52; Num. 18:15; 35:31–32; Isa. 35:10; 51:11.

243. Isa. 52:13–53:12 [esp. 53:10]; cf. 1 Tim. 2:5–6.

244. Malina and Rohrbaugh, *Social-Science Commentary on the Synoptic Gospels*, 246.

245. Lev. 21:18; 2 Sam. 5:8.

246. 1QSa 2:8–9.

247. Christopher D. Marshall, *Faith as a Theme in Mark's Narrative* (SNTSMS 64; Cambridge: Cambridge Univ. Press, 1989), 128.

248. See Ex. 22:26–27; Deut. 24:12–13.

249. See Num. 19:2; Deut. 21:3; 1 Sam. 6:7.

250. *m. Sanh.* 2:5.

251. *b. Sanh.* 98a.

252. Hanukkah; 1 Macc. 13:51; 2 Macc. 10:7; *m. Sukkah* 3:9.

253. Josephus, *J.W.* 2.17.8 § 434.

254. Mal. 3:1–2, cited in Mark 1:2.

255. Kathleen and Leon Ritmeyer, "Reconstructing Herod's Temple Mount in Jerusalem," *Archaeology in the World of Herod, Jesus, and Paul* (Washington: Biblical Archaeology Society, 1990), 2:43–45.

256. Pliny, *Nat. Hist.* 16.49.

257. Isa. 28:3–4; Jer. 8:13; Hos. 9:16; Joel 1:7, 12; Mic. 7:1; Hab. 3:17–18.

258. Jostein Ådna, "The Attitude of Jesus to the Temple," *Mishkan* 17–18 (1992–93): 68.

259. Josephus, *Ant.* 15.11.5 § 412.

260. Benjamin Mazar, "The Royal *Stoa* in the Southern Part of the Temple Mount," in *Recent Archaeology in the Land of Israel*, ed. H. Shanks (Washington/Jerusalem: Biblical Archaeology Society, 1984), 141–47.

261. *m. Šeqal.* 1:3; 4:7–8.

262. *t. Šeqal.* 1:6.

263. *m. Ker.* 1:7.

264. Josephus, *Ag. Ap.* 2.8 §106.

265. *m. Ber.* 9:5.

266. 1 Sam. 1:1–28; 1 Kings 8:27–51; Dan. 6:10.

267. *b. Ber.* 32b.

268. Josephus, *J.W.* 6.5.3 §§ 300–309.

269. Meier, *A Marginal Jew*, 164.

270. 4Q500 (4QBenediction); J. M. Baumgarten, "4Q 500 and the Ancient Conception of the Lord's Vineyard," *JJS* 40 (1989): 1–6.

271. See S. R. Llewellyn, "The Lease Agreement and the Parable of the Wicked Tenants," *New Documents Illustrating Early Christianity* (Sydney: Macquarie University, 1992): 88–107.

272. See 1 Kings 14:18; 15:29; 18:36; 2 Kings 9:36; 10:10; 14:25; Jer. 7:25; Dan. 9:6; Amos 3:7.

273. 2 Chron. 24:18–19; 36:15–16; Neh. 9:26.

274. 4Q Florilegium 1:11 on 2 Sam. 7:11; 1QSa 2:11–12 on Ps. 2:7.

275. Deut. 28:26; Jer. 7:33; 8:1; Ezek. 6:5; 29:5; 39:17; see Jer. 22:19, "He will have the burial of a donkey—dragged away and thrown outside the gates of Jerusalem."

276. Josephus *J.W.* 2.8.1 § 118; idem *Ant.* 18.1.1 §§ 1–10.

277. P. C. Finney, "The Rabbi and the Coin Portrait (Mark 12:15b, 16): Rigorism Manqué," *JBL* 112 (1993): 629–44.

278. *b. ʿAbod. Zar.* 54b.

279. See Acts 23:8; Josephus, *Ant.* 18.1.4 §§ 16–17; idem *J.W.* 2.8.14 §§ 164–65; *b. Nid.* 70b.

A similar story in *Qoh. Rab.* 5.10 § 1 has a Samaritan (who also relied only on the Pentateuch) asking questions to ridicule belief in the resurrection.

280. See also Wisd. Sol. 2:1–5.

281. *b. Mak.* 23b.

282. *b. Mak.* 24a.

283. Ephraim E. Urbach, *The Sages: Their Concepts and Beliefs* (Jerusalem: Magnes, 1975), 1:343–65.

284. See Ex. 22:21–23; Deut. 10:17; 24:17; Isa. 1:17, 23; 10:1–4; Ezek. 22:7.

285. *m. Šeqal.* 6:5–6.

286. *m. Šeqal.* 6:6; *t. Šeqal.* 3:8.

287. *Lev. Rab.* 3.5.

288. Philo, *Embassy* 294–97.

289. Kathleen and Leon Ritmeyer, "Reconstructing Herod's Temple," 45, 48.

290. Josephus, *J.W.* 6.1.1 §§ 5–7.

291. Josephus, *J.W.* 6.5.4. § 312.

292. Ibid., 2.13.4 §§ 258–60.

293. See Dan. 9:27; 11:31; 12:11; see also 1 Macc. 1:54.

294. See Josephus; *Ant.* 18.8.2–9 §§ 257–309; Philo, *Embassy*; Tacitus *History* 5.9.

295. Josephus, *J.W.* 4.3.7 §§ 151–54; 4.3.10 § 162; 4.5.4 §§ 341–43.

296. Ibid., 6.6.1 § 316.

297. "Blessed is the one who reads . . . this" in Rev. 1:3 refers to the public reader.

298. Dan. 8:15–17; 9:22; see also Mark 11:23; 12:10; see Rev. 1:3.

299. Ernest Best, "The Gospel of Mark: Who is the Reader?" *IBS* 11 (1989): 129.

300. Eusebius, *Eccl. Hist.* 3.5.11, 32.

301. Josephus, *J.W.* 6.5.2 §§ 285–87.

302. Dio Chrysostom, *Orations* 66.6–2–3.

303. Josephus, *J.W.* 4.7.5 §§ 433–36.

304. Ibid., 4.4.5 §§ 286–87.

305. Ibid., 6.3.5 §§ 214–19.

306. Ibid., 6.5.1 § 276; 6.6.3 §§ 354–55.

307. Nahman Avigad, "The Burnt House Captures a Moment in Time," in *Archaeology in the World of Herod, Jesus, and Paul*; vol. 2, ed. Hershel Shanks and Dan P. Cole (Washington: BAS, 1990), 96–104.

308. Josephus, *J.W.* 6.8–10 §§ 374–442.

309. Ibid., 6.8.5 § 408.

310. Crispin H. T. Fletcher-Louis, "The Destruction of the Temple and the Relativization of the Old Covenant: Mark 13:31 and Matthew 5:18," in *"The Reader Must Understand": Eschatology in Bible and Theology*, ed. K. E. Brower and M. W. Elliott (Leicester: Apollos, 1997), 145–69.

311. S. R. Llewelyn and R. A. Kearsley eds., *New Documents Illustrating Early Christianity*, ed. (Sydney: Macquarie University, 1992), 60.

312. Ex. 12:1–20; 23:15; 34:18.

313. See 2 Chron. 35:17; Josephus, *Ant.* 14.2.1 §21; 17.9.3 § 213.

314. Henri Daniel-Rops, *Daily Life in the Time of Jesus* (Ann Arbor: Servant, 1980), 96.

315. See Deut. 28:40; Ruth 3:3; Ps. 23:5; Eccl. 9:7–8; Ezek. 16:9; Dan. 6:15; Micah 6:15; Judith 16:7–8; *b. Šabb.* 41a, 61a; *b. Soṭah* 11b; *b. Ketub.* 66b.

316. See *Jub.* 49:10–12.

317. Rousseau and Arav, *Jesus and His World*, 341.

318. William Barclay, *The Gospel of Mark* (Philadelphia: Westminster, 1956), 347–48.

319. Cf. 9:1; Luke 2:26; John 21:23.

320. Meier, *A Marginal Jew*, 2.307.

321. Raymond E. Brown, *The Death of the Messiah* (New York: Doubleday, 1994), 1:123.

322. *m. B. Qam.* 7:7.

323. *y. ʿErub.* 10:1, 26a.

324. Juvenal, *Satire* 9.170–178.

325. Brown, *The Death of the Messiah*, 1:137.

326. Joan F. Taylor, "The Garden of Gethsemane Not the Place of Jesus' Arrest," *BAR* 21 (1995): 26–35, 62.

327. Ibid., 34.

328. Ibid., 35, citing Egeria, *Itinerarium* 36.2; and Theodosius, *De Sittu Sanctae* 10.

329. Brown, *The Death of the Messiah*, 1:167.

330. Joseph A. Fitzmyer, "Abba and Jesus' Relation to God," *À cause de l'évangile* (Paris: Cerf, 1985), 29–30.

331. James Barr, "'Abba' Isn't Daddy," *JTS* 39 (1988): 28–47.

332. Brown, *The Death of the Messiah*, 1:688.

333. Josephus, *J.W.* 2.20.7 § 581.

334. Josephus, *Ant.* 20.9.1 § 198.

335. *b. Pesaḥ.* 57a; *t. Menaḥ.* 13:21.

336. Josephus, *Ant.* 20.9.1 § 199.

337. Ibid., 18.2.2 §§ 34–35.

338. Zvi Greenhut, "Burial Cave of the Caiaphas Family," *BAR* 18/5 (1992): 28–36, 76; Ronnie Reich, "Caiaphas' Name Inscribed on Bone Boxes," *BAR* 18/5 (1992): 38–44, 76.

339. Josephus, *J.W.* 2.16.3 § 344.

340. *m. Sanh.* 1:6.

341. *y. Sanh.* 1.1, 18a. On the issue of Jewish power to carry out the death penalty, see Brown, *The Death of the Messiah*, 363–72.

342. Josephus, *Ant.* 20.9.1 §§ 200–203.

343. Josephus, *Ant.* 20.8.6 §§ 169–70.

344. See also *1 En.* 90:28–29.

345. See *2 Bar.* 4:2–6.

346. See Gen. 37:29; 2 Sam. 1:11; 2 Kings 18:37; 22:11–13; Isa. 37:1; Acts 14:14.

347. *b. Sanh.* 38b; *b. Ḥag.* 14a.

348. 4Q246.

349. David Flusser, "The Hubris of the Antichrist in a Qumran Fragment," *Judaism and the Origins of Christianity* (Jerusalem: Magnes, 1988), 210.

350. Josephus, *Ant.* 4.8.6 § 202.

351. *b. Sanh.* 93b citing Isa. 11:2–4.

352. David Flusser, "Who Is It That Struck You?" *Imm.* 20 (1986): 27–32.

353. *b. ʿErub.* 53b.

354. Geza Vermes, *Jesus the Jew* (Philadelphia: Fortress, 1973), 53.

355. Pliny, *Ep.* 10.96.3.

356. Ibid., 10.96.5.

357. Seneca, *On Anger* 2.7.3.

358. Brown, *The Death of the Messiah*, 1:629.

359. Peter Garnsey, "The Criminal Jurisdiction of Governors," *JRS* 58 (1968): 51–59.

360. Tacitus, *Ann.* 2.50; 3.38; Suetonius, *Tiberias* 58.

361. Josephus, *Ant. 17.10.8 §285.*

362. PFlor 1.61.59; cited by Deissmann, *Light*, 268–69.

363. *m. Pesah.* 8:6.

364. Suetonius, *Dom.* 11.

365. Philo, *Embassy* 299.

366. Suetonius, *Cal.* 19.

367. Josephus reports an incident when Herod came to the Sanhedrin "clothed in purple" (*Ant.* 14.9.4 § 173).

368. H. St. J. Hart, "The Crown of Thorns in John 19.2–5," *JTS* 3 (1952): 66–75.

369. Philo, *Flaccus* 6.36–41.

370. Nahman Avigad, "A Depository of Inscribed Ossuaries in the Kidron Valley, *IEJ* 12 (1962): 9–11.

371. Plutarch, *On the Delays of the Divine Vengeance* 554B.

372. Cicero *Rab. Post.* 5.16.

373. Quintilian, *Training in Oratory* 274.

374. Josephus, *J.W.* 5.11.1 §§ 449–451.

375. Joan E. Taylor, "Golgotha: A Reconsideration of the Evidence for the Sites of Jesus' Crucifixion and Burial," *NTS* 44 (1998): 180–203. See also Shimon Gibson and Joan E. Taylor, *Beneath the Church of the Holy Sepulchre: The Archaeology and Early History of Traditional Golgotha* (London: Palestine Exploration Fund, 1994).

376. Taylor, "Golgotha," 201.

377. Josephus, *J. W.* 5.4.1 § 146.

378. James H. Charlesworth, *Jesus Within Judaism: New Light from Exciting Archaeological Discoveries* (New York: Doubleday, 1988), 124.

379. Brown, *The Death of the Messiah*, 2:937–38, 1281–83. See Eusebius's account of the discovery of the tomb in *The Life of Constantine* 3.25–32.

380. *b. Sanh.* 43a.

381. Pliny, *Nat. Hist.* 14.15.

382. Wilhelm Michaelis, "σμυρνίζω," *TDNT*, 7:458–59.

383. T. E. Schmidt, "Mark 15.16–32: The Crucifixion Narrative and the Roman Triumphal Procession," *NTS* 41 (1995): 11–12.

384. Brown, *The Death of the Messiah*, 2:949.

385. Seneca, *Mor. Ep.* 101.12.

386. N. Haas, "Anthropological Observations on the Skeletal Remains from Giv'at ha-Mivtar," *IEJ* 20 (1970): 38–59; V. Tzaferis, "Jewish Tombs at and near Giv'at ha-Mivtar, Jerusalem," *IEJ* 20 (1970): 18–32; "Crucifixion—the Archeological Evidence," *BAR* 11/1 (1985): 44–53; J. Zias and E. Sekeles, "The Crucified Man from Giv'at ha-Mivtar—A Reappraisal," *IEJ* 35 (1985): 22–27; and Joe Zias and James H. Charlesworth, "Crucifixion: Archaeology, Jesus, and the Dead Sea Scrolls," *Jesus and the Dead Sea Scrolls*, ed. J. H. Charlesworth (New York: Doubleday, 1992), 273–89.

387. *LSJ*, 1983.

388. Frederick T. Zugibe, "Two Question About Crucifixion: Does the Victim Die of Asphyxiation? Would Nails in the Hands Hold the Weight of the Body?" *B Rev* 5/2 (1989): 34–43.

389. Horace, *Ep.* 1.16.48.

390. Seneca, *Ep.* 101.14.

391. Seneca, *To Marcia On Consolation* 20.3.

392. A. N. Sherwin-White, *Roman Society and Roman Law in the New Testament*, (Oxford: Clarendon, 1963), 46; Justinian, *Digest* 48.20.6.

393. *Gen. Rab.* 65:22; *Midr. Ps.* 11:7.

394. Ps. 35:21; 40:15; 70:3; 2 Kings 19:21; Job 16:4; Ps. 22:7; 109:25; Isa. 37:22; Jer. 18:16; Lam. 2:15; Sir. 12:18.

395. *b. Sukkah* 29a.

396. Philo, *Providence* 2:50.

397. Vergil, *Georgics* 1.463.

398. Joel 2:10; 3:14–15; Amos 5:18, 20; 8:9; see also Isa. 13:9–13; Jer. 15:9.

399. Gundry, *Mark*, 947.

400. *b. Ned.* 50a.

401. Plutarch, *Lives* 336, 1.7.

402. Zugibe, "Two Questions About Crucifixion: Does the Victim Die of Asphyxiation?" 34–43.

403. Ex. 26:37; 38:18; Num. 3:26.

404. Ex. 26:31–35; 27:16, 21; 30:6; 40:21; Lev. 16:2, 12–15; 21:23; 24:3.

405. *m. Šeqal.* 8:5.

406. Josephus, *J.W.* 5.5.4 §212–13.

407. Josephus, *J.W.* 6.5.3 §§ 293–95; see also *b. Yoma* 39b.

408. *b. Giṭ.* 56b.

409. Petronius, *Satyricon* 111.

410. Tae Hun Kim, "The Anarthrous υἱὸς θεοῦ in Mark 15, 39 and the Roman Imperial Cult," *Bib* 79 (1982): 238.

411. Raymond E. Brown, "The Burial of Jesus (Mark 15:42–47)," *CBQ* 50 (1988): 233–45.

412. Philo, *Flaccus* 83–84.

413. Philo, *Spec. Laws* 3.151–52.

414. Josephus, *J.W.* 4.5.2 § 317.

415. Rousseau and Arav, *Jesus and His World*, 167.

416. *t. ʾOhal.* 3:9.

417. Gabriel Barkay, "The Garden Tomb: Was Jesus Buried Here?" *BAR* 12/2 (1986): 40–57.

418. Gundry, *Mark*, 989.

419. See Dan. 7:9; Acts 1:10; 10:30; 2 Macc. 11:8–10.

420. Gen. 18:2; 19:1–3; Dan. 8:15–16; 9:21.

421. Josephus, *Ant.* 5.8.2 § 277.

422. Dan. 8:17–18; 10:8–12; Luke 2:10.

### *Sidebar and Chart Notes*

A-1. Ps. 103:19; Zech. 14:9.

A-2. *m. ʾAbot* 1:1.

A-3. Josephus, *J.W.* 3.10.8 §§ 516–21; see *Life* § 403.

A-4. L. I. Levine, "The Second Temple Synagogue: The Formative Years," in *The Synagogue in Late Antiquity*, ed. L. I. Levine (Philadelphia: Fortress, 1987), 7.

A-5. Josephus, *Ag. Ap.* 2.17 § 175.

A-6. On the debate over the date of this inscription, see Rainer Riesner "Synagogues in Jerusalem," in *The Book of Acts*, ed. Bauckham, 192–99.

A-7. Philo, *Dreams* 2.127.

A-8. See *1 En.* 12:3–4; 15:1; *2 Bar.* 2:1; 9:1–10:4.

A-9. See Dan. 7:13; *1 En.* 46–53.

A-10. Josephus, *Ag. Ap.* 2.27 §3.

A-11. Gen. 2:3; Ex. 20:8–11; 31:14; Deut. 5:12–15.

A-12. Ex. 31:14–15; 35:2; Num. 15:32–36.

A-13. *Mekilta Kaspa* 4 to Ex. 23:13.

A-14. *m. Ḥag.* 1:8.

A-15. *PGM* 4.1227–64, found in H. D. Betz, ed., *The Greek Magical Papyri in Translation*, 2d ed. (Chicago/London: Univ. of Chicago Press, 1992), 62.

A-16. See Matt. 14:1; Luke 3:19; 9:7.

A-17. Josephus, *Ant.* 17.18.1 § 188; 17.9.4 §§ 224–7l; 17.11.4 § 318; idem, *J. W.* 2.2.3 §§ 20–22; 2.6.3. §§ 93–95.

A-18. Ibid., *Ant.*, 18.7.1–2 §§ 240–56; idem, *J. W.* 2.9.6 §§ 181–83.

A-19. D. W. Chapman, *The Orphan Gospel: Mark's Perspective on Jesus* (The Biblical Seminar 16; Sheffield: JSOT, 1993), 186.

A-20. Lev. 11:44; 19:2.

A-21. Herbert Danby includes a synopsis of the rules of uncleanness from *Eliyahu Rabbah*, a commentary on the sixth division of the Mishnah *'Tohorot'* by Elijah, the Gaon of Wilna (*The Mishnah* [Oxford: Oxford Univ. Press, 1933], 800–804).

A-22. Jerome H. Neyrey, "The Idea of Purity in Mark's Gospel," *Semeia* 35 (1986): 92.

A-23. David H. Stern, *Jewish New Testament Commentary* (Clarksville, Md.: Jewish New Testament Publications, 1992), 92.

A-24. Daniel R. Schwartz, *Studies in the Jewish Background of Christianity* (WUNT 60; Tübingen: J. C. B. Mohr [Paul Siebeck], 1992), 64, citing a late midrash *Tanna Debe Eliyahu* 16.

A-25. H. Harrington, *The Impurity Systems of Qumran and the Rabbis: Biblical Foundations* (SBLDS 143; Atlanta: Scholars, 1993), 164. See *Jub.* 22:16; Acts 10:28.

A-26. *b. Soṭah* 4b.

A-27. *m. ʿEd.* 5:6.

A-28. *m. Ṭehar* 7:8; *b. Šabb.* 14a; *b. Sukkah* 26b; see Ex. 30:19, 21; 40:31.

A-29. *m. Yad.* 3:1; *m. Zabim* 5:12; *m. Parah* 11:5; *m. Soṭah* 5:2; *m. Ṭehar* 2:2.

A-30. David E. Garland, *Mark* (NIVAC; Grand Rapids: Zondervan, 1996), 316.

A-31. Ibid.

A-32. Cited by Martin Hengel, *The Zealots* (Edinburgh: T. & T. Clark, 1989), 277.

A-33. *m. Giṭ.* 9:3.

A-34. Yigael Yadin, *Bar-Kokhba* (London: Weidenfeld and Nicolson, 1978), 239.

A-35. Ibid., 222.

A-36. Josephus, *Ag. Ap.* 2.8 §§ 102–7.

A-37. Josephus, *J.W.* 5.5.6 §§ 222–24. On the whole description of the temple, see *J.W.*

5.5.1–6 §§ 184–226; and *Ant.* 15.11.3 §§ 391–402.

A-38. Timothy J. Geddert, *Watchwords: Mark 13 in Markan Eschatology* (JSNTSup 26; Sheffield: JSOT, 1989), 283, n. 53.

A-39. Garland, *Mark*, 505.

A-40. Morna D. Hooker, *The Gospel According to Saint Mark* (BNTC; Peabody, Mass.: Hendrickson, 1991), 302.

A-41. *b. Sanh.* 43a.; see also *t. Sanh.* 10:11; *y. Sanh.* 7:12.

A-42. Num. 35:30; Deut. 17:6; 19:15; *m. Sanh.* 4:1.

A-43. *m. Sanh.* 11:6; Deut. 19:16–21.

A-44. *m. Mid.* 5:4; *m. Sanh.* 11:2.

A-45. Tacitus, *An.* 3.38; 4.41, 57; Suetonius, *Tiberias* 41, 58; Cassius Dio, *Roman History* 58.2, 7; 3.8.

A-46. Philo, *Embassy* 24, 159–61.

A-47. Josephus, *J.W.* 2.9.3–4 § 175–77; *Ant.* 18.3.2 §§ 60–62.

A-48. Josephus, *Ant.* 18.4.1 §§ 85–87.

A-49. Ibid., 18.4.2 §§ 88–89.

A-50. Philo, *Embassy* 24, 159–61.

A-51. Ibid., 299–305.

A-52. Josephus, *Ant.* 18.6.5 §§ 174–78.

A-53. Jerry Camery-Hoggatt, *Irony in Mark's Gospel: Text and Subtext* (SNTSMS 72; Cambridge: Cambridge Univ. Press, 1991), 170–71.

A-54. Joel Marcus, *The Mystery of the Kingdom of God* (SBLDS 90; Atlanta: Scholars, 1986), 117.

# CREDITS FOR PHOTOS AND MAPS

CPSIA information can be obtained at www.ICGtesting.com
Printed in the USA
LVOW03s1932250615

443851LV00004B/9/P

9 780310 522911